JOURNEY
TO THE
LIGHT

FINDING OUR PLACE IN THE UNIVERSE THROUGH
THE SCIENCE OF NEAR-DEATH EXPERIENCES

BRIAN PICCHI

Tan Ru Nomad, LLC

JOURNEY TO THE LIGHT
Finding Our Place in the Universe through
the Science of Near-Death Experiences

Copyright © 2022 by Brian Picchi

Cover Design by Buzz Erlinger-Ford

Published by
Tan Ru Nomad, LLC
www.tanrunomad.com

ISBN: 9798809082150 (Paperback)

"The privilege of a lifetime is to become who you truly are."

—Carl Jung

Contents

Preface

Is there life after death? Does our consciousness live on? Do we have a purpose? These questions are deeply rooted in us. All of us seek answers to them, whether through religion, science, or journeys of self-discovery. Yet the questions are not new. They have been asked since the dawn of human existence. Ultimately, it comes down to determining whether our consciousness is a unique gift planted in us by an unknown force or simply the result of a long chain of seemingly random cosmic and evolutionary events. It's easy to see this as just another mystery of the universe that will probably remain unsolved until the moment of our death. I have grappled with questions like these for most of my life. I mean most of us have, right? However, because the answers to these questions are not scientifically confirmable, it suggests they are entirely driven by one's own faith. So is that really true? Our society is more evidence-based than ever before. Is there any real evidence for consciousness surviving into an afterlife? Well, as it turns out, there is! We call them near-death experiences (NDEs).

At a high level, NDEs can be described as supernatural events that many people claim happened to them while they were having a cardiac arrest. Even though we once dismissed them as hallucinations manifested entirely in the brain, we now know there is much more going on than that. Best of all, the sheer volume of case studies and research now available makes proving this easier than ever before.

As medical techniques greatly evolved starting back in the late twentieth-century, larger numbers of people were able to be resuscitated during life-threatening conditions, such as heart attacks, drowning, or other seemingly fatal events. A growing number of these survivors were claiming that they experienced incredible things before being revived. There were only a few people conducting research on this topic at that time, of whom Dr. Raymond Moody was the most famous. His 1975 book, *Life after Life,* was groundbreaking and is still studied and revered to this day. It was in many ways our first access to reliable and objective documentation on this subject. It was also a great relief to the many people who had this amazing experience happen to them but were too scared to talk about it for fear they'd be seen as crazy.

What was remarkable was that the things people saw and the sensations they felt were being echoed by others from around the globe. The core themes in all of their descriptions were identical. While we think of these types of experiences as a fairly recent trend, there is evidence they've been occurring for centuries, as seen through prehistoric burial sites and in some of our oldest literature. For example, ancient Greek philosophers documented hearing stories of NDEs over 2,000 years ago, and some of their greatest works were directly inspired by them. In his *Republic,* written around 375 BC, Plato writes about a warrior named Er who dies in battle, then experiences the afterlife in the cosmos before returning to his body.

That I would become a researcher and write a book on this topic is ironic because I have always been a very logical and scientifically-minded person. I grew up agnostic and with a strong fascination with our natural world and the universe around us. I remember spending hours as a five-year-old boy with the pages of *Time-Life Nature Library* books spread open on our family room floor, mesmerized by what I saw. The books were dated, even back then, but they were my first glimpse into the world of science.

The evolution of the human species was one of the topics that I took particular interest in. I ended up majoring in psychology with a focus on neuropsychology, becoming fascinated by the anatomy of the human brain and how neurotransmitters and chemicals influence the sensations that we experience. I've always relied on science for most of my beliefs. While I had heard of NDEs from an early age, I always just assumed the person was in a state of psychosis. My education in neuroscience helped cement this belief.

So what changed? Well, one day, by pure chance, I sat down and watched someone share their NDE from end-to-end. Now, this wasn't in a movie. It wasn't even really an interview. It was just one person speaking to the camera, unfiltered and in their own words. They talked about floating above their body in the operating room and seeing one of the nurses run down the hall in tears, screaming that she had killed him. Another spirit united with his to comfort him before venturing to a heavenly dimension. Their account was so detailed, and their delivery was so authentic that they were either telling the truth or it was an Oscar-worthy performance. That was the single moment that piqued my interest. I thought, "Wow! What if this was real?" I just had to hear another, and so I did. Soon, I found myself binge-watching several accounts a day. Some of these were on Bill Taylor's YouTube channel. Bill was the former president of the International Association for Near-Death Studies

(IANDS), who had an NDE himself and filmed many near-death survivors share their stories. Some other great content includes interviews by Mel Van Dusen in his series *Present!* as well as *NDE Radio*, a weekly show hosted by Lee Witting. So folks, put Netflix and Hulu on hold for a moment. This stuff will change your life!

After I had watched several dozen videos online, I started reading books written by both the survivors of NDEs and the doctors who studied in this field. Then, it was onto the research papers where I could see actual statistics and observations from more objective sources. Finally, I started to reach out and speak to some of these special individuals to hear their stories firsthand. I now believe with every fiber of my being that this phenomenon is absolutely real. I began to write down my observations from these videos and literature with theories of my own as to how everything connected based on scientific laws, psychology, and astronomy. What started as a personal journal eventually became something I decided I should share publically.

The main goal of this book is to summarize the major phases of the NDE, and through a deductive chain of reasoning, provide concrete evidence for their legitimacy. There is also a more philosophical purpose—discovering why we are here.

In studying so many NDEs in great detail, the parallels between these stories are striking. In summary, some of the more frequently reported events include out-of-body experiences (OBEs), the feeling of unconditional love and acceptance, traveling through a tunnel toward a light, walking in a beautiful field, meeting with God, seeing their life review, communicating with deceased loved ones and other spiritual beings, and returning to their bodies with newfound knowledge and abilities. Professional researchers have essentially seen this same basic paradigm throughout the world in every culture for decades now.

This book will mostly be divided into chapters that represent what I feel are the most significant phases of the person's NDE, as well as other tangential concepts that may be linked to the afterlife, such as past lives, religion, and dreams. For each chapter, I will describe the phase, provide examples from real cases, and apply scientific concepts along with my own theories to help make sense of them. Most literature about NDEs that involve science uses it as a way to disprove it. Mine goes the other way by using observable evidence and scientific reasoning to prove our consciousness survives us. Lots of the people mentioned in this book have documented their experiences in their own books or online videos and can be easily found if you wish to learn more about a particular case. Because of the complexity of their experiences, some of their stories have been split up to focus more clearly on one particular NDE pattern at a time. This will help us explore each phase individually, like pieces of a puzzle, ultimately revealing the complete picture of the afterlife and how we are connected to the universe. Any attempt of mine to interpret these events or draw conclusions about them comes from a place of logic and respect for those who were brave enough to share them.

The difficulty in putting the events of an NDE into chapters is that each person may only experience some of the possible phases and in their own sequence. Each case is deeply personal and yet, at the same time, extremely similar to others. For instance, some report having a life review with God in a divine light after traveling through a tunnel. Others claim that their life review took place in a completely different location all by themselves. On Earth, we have a tendency to break things down into linear stages with clear separations between them. In an NDE, things can sometimes blend together and jump in different orders.

Regardless of the sequence and number of phases experienced, there is no denying the consistency of detail and the personal truth of these stories. That being said, even if one believes their authenticity, there is a difference between a personal truth and an objective truth. Someone can believe wholeheartedly that what they saw and felt were real, but how do you measure that in an empirical way? While parts of their experience can't be proven, other parts can. In fact, there is so much evidence these days that any reasonable person would have to believe them, or soon they may be the ones looked at as fools.

Even so, the entire premise of consciousness surviving our mortal bodies seems to conflict with nature. If we can't see or measure it, then how do we prove something exists? Yet the laws of physics and thermodynamics are clear in that energy cannot be created or destroyed, it can only be transformed. When our physical bodies die, the energy that made them up changes, getting recycled to provide fuel for other life to spring forward, aka the circle of life. So what happens to the energy of our consciousness? That's really what the debate is all about, isn't it? If consciousness is merely a property of our physical biology, and thus confined to our human body, then that's that. Show's over. But if it is separate from the body, then that energy must go someplace. So where does it go? That's where near-death research comes into play.

Skeptics have many theories to explain away near-death phenomena, ranging from mistaking the light at the end of the tunnel for the overhead light above the operating table to neurotransmitters and chemicals being released as the body shuts down that makes the person feel a psychedelic euphoria.

Skepticism is a good thing, but there comes the point when there is just too much evidence to ignore, particularly when so many people from completely different cultures witness the exact same things, their accounts can be corroborated, and some of the reports come from third-party eyewitnesses who are in perfect health. For instance, with 100 percent accuracy, many patients have described all of the conversations and actions in their operating rooms as well as other rooms in a hospital while their bodies are unconscious. There are patients who, while on the other side, meet siblings they had never seen before because they were adopted or died before their time. There are physicians and nurses who physically see the spirit leave a newly deceased person right before their eyes. There are even completely healthy bystanders who literally share the experience of the dying person, traveling to the light with them and watching as they reunite with their loved ones and wave goodbye.

The world in between our lives is a fascinating and wonderful place. However, NDEs do so much more than just paint a picture of heaven—they show us the path of our human destiny, how we can influence the universe, and how we can discover our best, unique versions of ourselves.

A remarkable fringe benefit of researching NDEs was that it helped me overcome my long battle with severe obsessive-compulsive disorder (OCD). Having OCD tendencies is like having a force inside of you that tries to take control, influencing your behavior, resulting in a power struggle for your own identity. It is much the same for people with addictions or phobias. You feel helpless, like a passenger in your own body, bending to the will of irrational thought and allowing it to hold you back from reaching your full potential. Knowing that there is an afterlife and hearing the messages brought back from those who've been there has brought me clarity and peace of mind that helped me discover my true self and what was really important. I was finally able to put aside my stress and start to enjoy life to the fullest, knowing that everything was going to work out fine.

We can't control the environment around us, but we can control how we respond to it. We can choose how to process things and treat other people. There was something else that I noticed, too. The people I shared these stories with became much less anxious and judgmental. I saw a kinder and more beautiful person in their place.

As we journey to the light together through the eyes of the incredible people who took this trip, I ask that you hear their stories with an open mind and an open heart. You might just be amazed.

CHAPTER ONE

History and Introduction

A hundred thousand years ago, there was an ancient culture that lived near the Mediterranean Sea in modern-day Israel. They buried their loved ones in two caves known as Qafzeh and Es-Skhul. Both the young and the old were laid to rest there, accompanied by stone tools, animal bones, and seashell necklaces painted in red ochre. One man was placed with the jawbone of a wild boar positioned on his chest with his hands made to grip it.[1,2] What did this signify? Was this man a great hunter? Was it to provide him good fortune in the next life?

Our fascination with the afterlife stretches back to our earliest human ancestors, who went to great lengths to honor their own. At a time when survival was everything and resources were precious, we risked our lives acquiring rare elements, forging weapons, and producing jewelry only to leave them with our loved ones in their tombs. It seems impractical to waste resources in this way, and yet it was something very important to us. We knew our human bodies were temporary, so perhaps we also considered our possessions temporary, ultimately destined to be returned back to the Earth, or to accompany us in our voyage to the cosmos.

These practices continued through the ages, only the burial demonstrations became much more elaborate and decorative. One example of this is the Sungir caves of Russia, where around 35,000 years ago, an adult man and two children were adorned with 13,000 ivory beads made from mammoth tusks. Archeologists estimate it would have taken some 10,000 hours of labor to produce.[3]

Theories vary as to the true motivations of ancient cultures like these, but I like to imagine that it means we held deep, spiritual beliefs about the afterlife—that we knew there was more to life than the physical reality we saw.

However, it wasn't until the Neolithic age began around 9,500 BC that our species truly made their voices heard. This period of our history is celebrated as the time when we started to first lay the seeds of modern civilization with larger communities and early farming practices. It was also a period defined by the complex stone structures that were built, like Stonehenge in England, Newgrange in Ireland, and Gobekli Tepe in Turkey. They were not built for housing, education, or government purposes. They were designed to align perfectly with celestial objects in our sky. One might be tempted to label these structures what today would be called astronomical observatories, but for them, they were much more than places to stargaze. They also used them to honor their deceased loved ones since they served as burial grounds, too. These sites may have been thought to facilitate the transition of the soul into the afterlife. We and the stars seemed interconnected. This pairing also included our closest star: the sun.

Take Newgrange, for example. Almost ten centuries before the Great Pyramid of Giza, there was an ancient culture in Ireland that built this wonderful structure around 3,200 BC. Once a year, during the winter solstice, the morning sun rises and shines through a perfectly positioned roof box that illuminates a pathway deep into the cave structure, reaching the inner chamber where several human bodies were deposited. The whole event lasts for only about fifteen minutes. One current belief is that the light was intended to guide the soul outside the cave to be delivered to their spirit ancestors. I can say from personal experience that standing inside the walls of that ancient chamber and briefly renting that still air as the light pierced through to me was a deeply spiritual experience.

We were also fascinated by the planets. The word "planet" itself comes from the ancient Greeks, who called them *planetes asteres,* meaning "wandering stars," since they moved relative to other stars. The ancient Romans named most of our planets after gods they thought resembled them, such as blood-stained Mars for their god of war and the brightest planet Venus for their goddess of love and beauty.

The ancient Egyptians believed that their souls traveled to the stars of Orion, which is associated with Osiris, their god of death, rebirth, and the afterlife. One theory goes so far as to claim the three pyramids of Giza were intentionally positioned to align to the three stars of Orion's belt and that the star shafts that were built in the burial chambers were designed to allow the soul a pathway to the stars.

With such a long history of these practices, it should come as no surprise that we as human beings are still quite curious about this topic. Fortunately for us, we are closer than ever to unraveling these age-old mysteries. The breakthrough happened in the 1960s as advancements in medical knowledge led to greater numbers of patients being revived after having a cardiac arrest. Some of these patients described experiencing supernatural phenomena during their unconscious state. While these types of experiences have likely been happening for untold centuries, only very recently have they been thoroughly documented. As a result, communities like IANDS had formed, and a term was created to define this experience. Dr. Raymond Moody called this phenomenon a near-death experience, and the people who have them are sometimes called NDE-ers. The term itself could be seen as a bit of a misnomer since most people who have them didn't nearly die—they did die. Perhaps a more accurate term is a temporary death experience. Regardless, the expression has stuck, and that is a good thing because it gives us a consistent frame of reference. By the late 1980s and early '90s, the term was fairly commonplace, and one could regularly see NDE-ers share their stories on daytime talk shows with Geraldo Rivera, Phil Donahue, and Oprah. In the digital age, we can communicate with more people than ever before to share our experiences, beliefs, and knowledge.

So just how many people have had an NDE, anyway? Well, the number is far greater than anyone could have predicted, with Gallup Poll results over the decades showing that as many as one in every twenty-five people in the US alone has experienced them.[4,5] The European Academy of Neuropsychology had researchers from thirty-five countries recently report even higher percentages.[6]

One researcher named Dr. Penny Satori has found that those numbers might even be underreported. During her time as a nurse practitioner, she became very interested in the topic and conducted her own research on NDEs. In a five-year study published in 2008, she interviewed many Intensive Care Unit patients from several hospitals. There were fifteen people who reported to her their experiences of having an NDE. However, only two of them volunteered the information. The others had to be approached.[7] Of course, this is a relatively small sample, so the evidence is anecdotal, but it does suggest there may be many more cases out there than we know about.

Some of these special individuals have shared their profound stories publicly, while many choose to keep their experience private for themselves and their families, seeing it as a sacred event. Even those that do go public sometimes wait years before doing so. Part of the reason for the delay is that they find it hard to put into words what heaven is like. They say things, such as "feels like home," "more real than here," "unconditional love and forgiveness," and "indescribably beautiful." They recall seeing flowers, trees, and rivers that beam with light and life. They say our souls also beam with light. There is a feeling of recognition that they have been to this place many times before and that it is their real home. Life and death on Earth are an illusion because we are eternal souls exploring the human experience.

One woman named Martha St. Claire had a profound NDE in her early twenties while water skiing. She described our souls as "beautiful beings of light." She also said that we can still connect to our loved ones who have crossed over and that the place we go to and our very essence transcends religion and other human conditions.[8]

Another case involved a man named Jang Jaswal. He described having every one of his senses filled with love and said that his previously turbulent mind was now at total and complete peace. He said the Sanskrit word *shanti* was the best term he could come up with to describe this sensation. It translates to "cosmic peace."[9]

In a unique case later to be explored, a young man named Scott Taylor traveled to the light with his deceased girlfriend and her young son together in a shared death experience. They went on while he was returned to his body.[10]

His description of the account is one of the best that I have heard, not in terms of the details of what he saw, but rather in how the experience was, in his words, "ineffable", meaning it is beyond human description. He says that "words put boundaries on things," so when one attempts to describe what they see using human language and with only our five senses, the person listening to their NDE creates their own interpretation, which doesn't begin to describe the event. Scott visually recognized his loved ones, but he also identified them through their patterns of energy.

Many have described this heightened awareness while on the other side as an internal feeling whereby they can sense the souls around them and view their energy signatures. This ability also enables communication to be accomplished entirely through thought waves.

Before we move onto the detailed chapters ahead, I'd like to share one specific NDE as sort of an ice breaker to give you a sense of what a so-called "classic near-death experience" is like. This individual was filmed by the aforementioned Bill Taylor. She experienced just some of the phases of the total possible, which is quite common. Here is a brief summary of her account:

In 1977, a twenty-year-old woman travelled out west with her friends on vacation. On one of the days she was on an inner tube riding down a huge irrigation ditch. She did this several times and on her last round, she fell and found herself tumbling uncontrollably in circles underneath the water. She held her breath for as long as she could, but ultimately drowned. She then found herself in a dark room with soft, velvet-like walls. She looked up and saw a pinpoint of light in the far distance. Drawn to it, she moved in its direction. As she started moving faster toward the light, she was suddenly overcome with the feeling of unconditional love and knowing that everything was going to be okay. Eventually, the small point of light grew larger and larger until she could clearly see that it was a large ball of energy that was brighter than the sun. It was a gentle light, and she could look right at it. She collided with this energy, and the feeling of absolute love and acceptance overwhelmed her, like a cup that was overflowing. Eventually, she detached and stood right in front of the light. The light was God.

God communicated with her telepathically. The communication was instant, meaning that she didn't have to even complete her thought before a reply was received. She asked many of the big questions that any of us would likely ask in her situation and received answers to all of them. While she would retain the knowledge of her experience in great detail, it was made clear that the universal knowledge she was receiving was temporary.

God then told her that they were going to look at her life. Her attention was directed toward what she described as something similar to a television screen. She was shown every moment of her life from birth until death. However, it wasn't like watching a film. She was actually reliving every single moment. She viewed her life with a new sense of realism, including experiencing the events from the perspective of whoever she was interacting with. She felt their visceral reactions to her words and actions. She felt the impact that she had on them and how that, in turn, impacted the way that person treated others.

Within her life review, there were certain pivotal moments that she and other NDE-ers describe as "learning events". These are moments where you did something that elicited very intense emotional responses and impacted others greatly. For her, one of the moments was when she was fourteen, and her grandmother had to stay with her family temporarily. She had to give up her room and she was bitter about that. One day, her grandmother fell down just outside her room and hit her head against the wall, causing the wall to break. She laughed at her grandmother. She could now feel the pain this caused her. It was enough for her to feel great regret and shame for doing it. There were also moments of tremendous joy that she could relive and could feel and see the positive impact that her kindness brought to others.

It should be made clear that she felt no judgment from God for any of these actions. She claimed, as others have, that God simply discusses what lessons were learned through these events, but he does not judge or punish the individuals. They feel only warmth and immeasurable love from him. In fact, she and God laughed at the silly moments and the times when she took life too seriously.

After the review was over, she was told that it wasn't her time yet and that she now had to return to her body. She resisted and supplicated for God to let her stay. This place was too magnificent to leave behind. They playfully argued about this until God directed her attention below to the Earth and projected a scene in which her family learned about her death. She felt their pain and sorrow; therefore, she quickly changed her mind. She asked if there was something she should do when she returned and was told that she should show love to everyone. Before she was ready to return to her life, she asked God for a favor. She requested if she could reconnect with him as they had done earlier when she first arrived. God answered, "Sure." They once again connected in a sweet, loving embrace, and her soul was once more enveloped in love and joy. She was whisked away and returned to her body in the water. God whispered, "Hold your breath just a little bit longer." Shortly after, she was rescued by one of her friends.

The event changed her almost immediately, inspiring her to be a better person. For a moment, she could even see auras around her friends. She felt compelled to hug each of them and let them know just how loved they are by God.[11]

Hopefully, this story gives you an idea of the type of experience and the long-lasting effects of an NDE. We are made to see the influence we have on others and the total forgiveness, acceptance, and understanding of God concerning events from our lives, the same way we can confide in a best friend or significant other without the risk of judgment or retaliation. While each experience is unique and special in their own way, they all follow a predictable pattern of one or more phases. We will now look closely at each of those phases and attempt to decipher their meaning and origin.

CHAPTER TWO

The Out-of-Body Experience

I magine opening your eyes to find yourself hovering several feet above the ground. At first, there is confusion as you try to process where you are and what is happening. It appears to be the emergency room in a hospital. Below you is a body with several people frantically trying to resuscitate whoever it is. You then remember being in a fatal accident. Your curiosity draws you closer to the body until you realize that it's you! Only for some reason, the sight doesn't frighten you. In fact, you feel at total and complete peace.

Meanwhile, the doctors and staff are panicking as they continue to perform on your body as they believe they have lost their patient. You try to communicate to them that everything is fine.

This is the OBE stage of an NDE and is typically the first phase experienced by a near-death survivor. It is also one of the most verifiable stages, as some of the other ones take place outside of our earthly realm, and thus are difficult to substantiate.

During this event, the person will sometimes retain full control of their movement and drift around the room, sometimes traveling through the nearby walls and ceilings to the adjoining rooms and floors. In some cases, they can seemingly teleport from one spot to another just by thought. Sometimes, this can even be to faraway locations, such as visiting their family in a different city or country.

Dr. Rajiv Parti, the Chief of Anesthesiology at Bakersfield Heart Hospital, described the OBE portion of his NDE, occurring just before Christmas in 2010. While floating above his body in the operating room at UCLA, his field of vision expanded to where he could see his family in India. He said, "My mom was wearing a green sari and a green sweater, and my sister was wearing blue jeans and a red sweater." The sister asked, "What should we make for dinner?" To this the mother replied, "Lentil sounds good." A couple of days after the surgery, he called them and confirmed his observation was correct.[1]

In some cases, the patient will float so high that they literally travel through our atmosphere into outer space. They report seeing the Earth similar to how astronauts see it from the International Space Station. One such patient was the famous Swiss psychologist, Carl Jung. At the age of sixty-nine, he suffered a heart attack while in a hospital and had his own NDE. His soul ascended into space, where he looked back and saw our planet. Here are some of his words describing this awesome experience:

"It seemed to me that I was high up in space. Far below, I saw the Earth, bathed in a gloriously blue light. I saw the deep blue sea and the continents. Far below my feet lay

Ceylon (Sri Lanka), and in the distance ahead of me, the subcontinent of India. My field of vision did not include the whole Earth, but its global shape was plainly distinguishable and the outlines shone with a silvery gleam through that wonderful blue light."

He went on to describe dark patches of green, the reddish-yellow Arabian Desert, cloud cover, and snow over the Himalayas. He concluded his description by saying, "The sight of the Earth from this height was the most glorious thing I'd ever seen."

What makes his account all the more incredible is that his description of Earth from that vantage point was spot on, and yet it happened in 1944. It would be another two decades before we would take our first color photos of Earth from that altitude.[2]

In fact, these days, with commercial space flights, it seems that anyone with enough money or connections can travel to this point of apogee above our atmosphere to experience this amazing view. This is because space travel now exists in the private sector, with companies such as SpaceX and Blue Origin taking civilian-only crews into space using reusable rockets. In 2021, a team of four, including a ninety-year-old William Shatner, flew aboard a Blue Origin rocket. The man who portrayed the intrepid captain of a starship for so many years and inspired many to pursue careers in scientific fields was now a space traveler in real life. He described the blackness of space and the vibrant blue of Earth as the "boundary between life and death."[3]

Those who float above their bodies with these OBEs transcend whatever physical condition they were previously in, be it limited mobility or something affecting their senses. Even the blind have reported this hovering phase of the NDE in what is sometimes their first time seeing the world.

One blind woman named Vicki Umipeg Noratuk reported how she was finally able to see. She only knew that it was her own body that she was looking at when she recognized her wedding ring and the curls and length of her own hair.[4]

In many cases, the person is accompanied by other spirits who float beside them. They sometimes communicate and see this spirit, while other times, they are simply comforted by their presence. One NDE-er named Barbara Bartolome described these spirits as "loving, accepting, and eternal."[5] Some see deceased relatives and communicate with them. The conversations are usually brief, and they are told that it is not yet their time and they must go back.

What is astonishing about all of this is that the person retains their consciousness, their memories, and even their personality through all of this, even while in an incorporeal form. When they are resuscitated, they recall every single moment while they were seemingly unconscious—every word that was spoken, every action that was taken, no matter how small or insignificant. Naturally, the doctors and nurses are a bit baffled and amazed by what they've heard, although with the increasing number of NDEs, some of them may have seen this happen before.

Now, I realize that for some of you, this whole OBE thing sounds ridiculous and extraordinary. It should. However, with literally thousands of OBE accounts documented, there clearly must be something going on. Still, that doesn't necessarily mean that they are real and the skeptic in me sometimes whispers a dictum from famous astronomer and childhood hero of mine, Carl Sagan, who said, "Extraordinary claims require extraordinary evidence." It's fairly obvious that the experiences being relayed are true and accurate for the people who had them. In other words, they aren't lying about having them. But how can we confirm these things actually happened? How do you quantitatively observe and prove someone's consciousness can float around outside of their body? Let me share some stories that will attempt to do just that.

In one of the most impressive cases, Dr. Norma Bowe from Kean University described an event involving a young woman who was rushed to the hospital after a serious car accident. She remained in a coma for months. Finally, she woke up one day and told the nurses in the room about experiencing the light and other classic NDE events. However, one of those observations stood out. She said while she was floating above her body, she saw everything that was happening in the room and even memorized the twelve-digit serial number written on the top of a seven-foot-tall respirator machine while in a coma. One of the nurses remarked, "Okay, so what's the number?" and proceeded to write it down. A few days later, while the patient was recovering, a maintenance worker came by to take the equipment back into storage when the nurse told him to hold on and asked if he could get a ladder and see if there was a number on top of it. The man seemed a bit puzzled but agreed. Sure enough, there was a serial number there—exactly twelve digits long and an identical match to the one the patient provided.[6] You can imagine the shock and awe on the nurses' faces.

Another case involves Robert Bare, a former police officer. This case also takes place in a hospital. During his cardiac arrest, he floated above his body and watched the medical staff try to revive him. While this was happening, he also saw a specific event happen in a different part of the hospital. His spirit witnessed two staff members who were going through his wallet, frantically looking for his insurance card. The staffers found his police ID, and one of them said, "Whoa, this guy is a retired highway patrolman!" Robert tried to talk to them to tell them where his insurance card was because it was in a special place, but of course, they couldn't hear him. After being resuscitated, he told the doctor about all of this. The doctor was very intrigued, so he called up the staff members who were trying to find his ID. Every detail was corroborated.[7]

In a somewhat famous story involving a blue tennis shoe, a patient named Maria floated above her body while on the second floor of the Harborview Medical Center. After a while, she continued to float up through the ceiling into the next floor and then through more ceilings until she was clear above the hospital's roof. She circled around the building and noticed a large, dark blue tennis shoe with white laces lying on a third-story overhang ledge on the other side of the hospital.

When she was later resuscitated, she told a social worker in the room named Kimberly Clark Sharp about her experience, including the shoe. Maria was very excited and emotional, so while reluctant at first, Kimberly decided to check it out just to calm her down. She went up to the third story to the window where the shoe was reported to be. Sure enough, the shoe was there, exactly as described, and in a location where it could not be seen from the ground. In fact, because of the isolated area where the hospital building was located and its height, the only way to see it would be from an aerial view.[8]

Keep in mind that this took place before commercial drones were a thing, so we can rule that out. Really, there are only a few possible explanations for this. One is that she somehow tossed the shoe up there herself before checking into the hospital, had a cardiac arrest, and then lied about it to the social worker as a prank. I could actually believe someone from the YouTube generation might think this was a good idea and try to pull it off for more views, but it just seems too far-fetched in this case. Besides, what would the pay-off be?

She didn't write any books or go on TV. She didn't even speak English. The next possibility is that she saw the shoe overhead in a plane or helicopter earlier, but it was confirmed that the hospital is not under a flight path. Maybe she was an amateur magician? Honestly, the only explanation that seems to make sense is that she saw it in spirit form exactly as she described.

While it is often the patient who decides to share their story, sometimes the physicians do as well. A more recent case was shared with Dr. Moody while doing a talk in Italy. The physician shared the details of an event where he was performing a routine procedure on a patient, when suddenly and unexpectedly, the patient went into cardiac arrest. He was not able to resuscitate him and was struggling to understand what had happened when the doors to the room flew open, and a screaming lady ran in. At first, he thought she was some crazy person, but then she calmed down enough to explain that her husband's spirit just told her that he was not dead. Sure enough, the patient slowly regained a steady heartbeat. When he was fully conscious again, he told the doctor that he had been floating in the room and tried to tell him that he was still there, but the doctor couldn't hear him, so he went through the wall into the waiting room and told his wife, who was able to hear him.[9]

There are lots of stories just like these that defy explanation. Medical associations have started to just accept them because the numbers are so high. The only logical way to interpret them is to believe them, and if they are telling the truth about this one aspect of their NDE, then perhaps there is also truth to the rest of their experiences. In fact, even if you dismiss everything else, this OBE phase alone is enough to prove our consciousness is a separate entity from our body.

Now for some who have an OBE, there is something

else that accompanies their experience. As they float around their surroundings, they are able to read the thoughts of everyone around. They'll hear the prayers of their family or see a doctor in the hall and know exactly what they are thinking and where they are going.

One of the people who has experienced this ability is Linda Jacquin who had an NDE at just four years old. She had been playing by a creek during a picnic and travelled too far into the water and drowned. Her spirit was lifted out of her body by her spirit guides. At one point during her experience, she was made to see her body. One man was trying to resuscitate her as her friends and family watched helplessly. She could read all of their minds and knew exactly what they were thinking. She could see sparkly orbs above their heads that represented the prayers they were making in that moment. Linda ultimately made the choice to return because she knew her older brother would need her guidance later in life.[10]

In another case, a man named Jeff Olsen had an NDE after being in a car accident. During his OBE, he could see every moment of every life he flew by. He described it like he knew them even though they were strangers. He saw one nurse who he could see was sexually and emotionally abused at a young age. How wonderful she was to now be in a hospital healing other people. He felt great love for everyone there.[11]

With all of these fascinating cases, you might wonder why there hasn't been more research done on this topic. Can we recreate these experiences in a controlled setting? Well, there actually has been progress in this area, although more studies would be great. The most recent and in-depth study concluded in 2015 and was called the AWARE (Awareness During Resuscitation) study. The idea was simple: verify that patients could truly retain consciousness and float above their bodies by placing targets on the tops of shelves near the ceiling in specific rooms. When a person is resuscitated, ask them what the image was on the target. There were also other objectives for the study, but for the purpose of this chapter, we will just focus on that particular element.

It was a study spanning several years involving 2,060 patients in fifteen hospitals across the United States, the United Kingdom, and Austria. Of them, only 140 survived well enough to be interviewed. Of those survivors, just nine of them had NDEs, and only two had an OBE. Just one of those two agreed to talk about their experience. While that one person did correctly describe the conversations and people who were in the room, they didn't see the target. They said they were simply too focused on everything else going on.[12] Remember that these patients didn't know about the target or volunteer for this study. They were often emergency patients, after all. Even if the patients were still conscious when being taken to the ER, the doctor's first priority is saving their life, not completing the study. Just imagine a physician saying, "Hey, if you happen to die during our procedure, would you mind floating over to the ceiling by that corner over there and looking at the target we placed there?"

In all seriousness, I still think it was a fascinating study, and I would love to see more research like it done in a controlled way. A single reported OBE is simply not enough to draw any conclusions. If there were fifty OBEs and none of them could identify the targets, then it would be a red flag. Of course, even if one day we have a study that is a success and all the patients correctly identify the targets, there will still be skeptics. That's okay. It will be only at the point of dying that they will truly understand.

It is hard to know just how long people have been experiencing OBEs, but some ancient artwork could suggest a long history of the phenomenon occurring. Throughout the world, we find ancient ground drawings made from earth and stone called geoglyphs. One of the most famous examples is the Nasca Lines of Peru made about 2,000 years ago. The images can be animals or humanoids that are only truly appreciated from aerial views high above the ground. Theories have been thrown around, ranging from burial grounds to aliens, but in truth, their purpose remains a mystery. One possibility to consider is that they were drawn as a beacon to attract the attention of spiritual beings. Maybe some members of these cultures had an OBE before being revived and shared their experience of floating high above the ground. With this revelation, the people may have started a practice of leaving the bodies of the deceased temporarily by these geoglyphs if an effort to draw their souls back into their bodies. It could also be a sign for other beings, such as angels, to follow to collect the spirits of the dead. In the end, we can only speculate, but before jumping on the ancient astronaut bandwagon, consider this theory, okay?

For some, the OBE phase is the only one that they experience, quickly being returned to their body as soon as they are resuscitated. For others, it is just the beginning of a long journey. Those that move on are often taken to a tunnel of light leading to a beautiful field. It is this experience of traveling to the light that we will look at next.

CHAPTER THREE

The Light at the End of the Tunnel

It is perhaps one of the most popular clichés regarding an NDE. You see examples of it all the time, especially in television and film. There will be a scene where a friend or family member is holding the hand of a loved one as they lie dying. They tell them calmly, "Go to the light." You might also hear, "Don't go to the light," if they want the person to come back. The expression has mostly been relegated to a joke, but where did it come from, and is there any truth to its origin?

It is while in the proverbial tunnel that people most often report seeing this light. This passageway is described similarly by seemingly everyone who has traveled it, although how they enter the tunnel can vary.

During their OBE, as the person's soul watches from above their physical body at the scene of an accident or in a hospital room, they are suddenly directed toward a tunnel.

They are told not to look back and to let go of their bond to the physical world. Some enter into this tunnel through a portal, while others must first wait in a dark void. This waiting room has walls made of velvet or felt material. Eventually, they'll see a distant light, emerging as a beacon. This is followed by an irresistible pull that moves their soul toward it as they begin to travel through the tunnel.

The tunnel is often described as circular, like a tube with spiral lights along the edges. As one moves closer to the divine light at the end of it, they feel the overwhelming sensations of love, beauty, and peace. Many sense billions of souls welcoming them home, and they are comforted by a feeling of recognition, as though they have made this trip countless times before. The speed at which the soul travels is extremely fast, with one former traveler saying they accelerated to what they intuitively knew was "the speed of light or conceivably faster."[1] There have also been reports of those claiming to go through colorful ring-like sections. Some have described each of these colors as representing different attributes of God with their own distinct feeling.

For many years, there was a theory that the tunnel we see is from our memory as a baby coming through the birth canal. However, there have been endless studies that reveal that people who had natural births report this experience at the same rate as those who had cesarean births.[2]

A more likely scenario that might best describe this experience is a concept we already know as theorized by astrophysicists and popularized in science fiction. Physicists Albert Einstein and Nathan Rosen appropriately called these tunnels the Einstein-Rosen bridges. We know them better as wormholes, and while they may only partially explain the physical concept of this phenomenon, it is a start. You can think of wormholes as theoretical doorways connecting two points of the universe together.

Imagine if you could fold a section of the universe like a piece of paper and touch two points together, such as the Earth and Titan. If you stab a straw through those two areas and pull the paper apart, then the connecting straw is your wormhole. Connecting these two worlds together means you could step out of one and onto the other. Depending on the size of the tunnel, it could be a very fast trip.

Applying this concept on a grander scale can offer even more possibilities, like connecting to some place in Alpha Centauri. While it may be our closest neighboring star system, it is still over four light-years away, yet it may only take mere minutes to get there. In those examples, the two points can actually be plotted in the physical universe, but what about connecting Earth to a completely different universe in another dimension. Could that be how our souls travel between Earth and heaven? Wormholes are unstable and temporary things for humans, yet they seem to be perfectly stable for the spirits who use them. Maybe the beings of the spiritual dimension have the technology or means to control them. The laws of physics claim that the fastest speed achievable for energy is the speed of light, so bending the fabric of the universe through wormholes seems to be the only scientific explanation.

What happens when we reach the light varies with different possibilities: Some meet with God or other spiritual beings. Some enter heaven. There have also been reports of seeing a physical barrier between themselves and the source of the light. That barrier is like a window with countless silhouettes moving on the other side.

What is remarkable about this portal is that it is not only NDE-ers who have seen it. There is a phenomenon called a shared death experience, sometimes referred to as an empathic near-death experience. It is when a second person accompanies the dying person to the light, and it is more common than you'd think. Let me provide a few such cases.

In one example, a medical professor named Dr. Denise Jean Jamieson had been staying with her aging mother. She returned one day from work to find her mother collapsed on the floor and not breathing. She performed CPR on her for several minutes until she finally accepted that she was gone. All of sudden, she found herself being lifted outside of her body. She was then looking down at her own body along with her now-deceased mother beside it. Suddenly, she saw her mother's spirit floating right by her. She noticed a bright light emanating from behind them. She described it like a breach in the universe that was pouring out light like water from a broken pipe. From this light came several spirits, some of whom Dr. Jamieson recognized as relatives and friends. The others, she assumes, were people before her time. The two said their final farewells, and all of the spirits were drawn back into the light, which then closed in the form of a spiral, similar to the shutter blades of a camera.[3]

Now, it is one thing for a skeptic of NDEs to dismiss such occurrences as something like oxygen deprivation or chemicals causing hallucinations. It's another thing entirely to have a perfectly healthy person experience the exact same events as the person who died.

In the previous chapter, you were introduced to Linda Jacquin. In addition to the NDE described earlier, she had another incredible event happen to her when she was seven years old. Back in the 1950s, she had just gotten eye surgery and had to stay overnight in the hospital. At that time, parents had to return home for overnight stays and this was the first time Linda had been separated from her family like this, and she felt scared and alone.

Both her eyes were bandaged up from the surgery, so she couldn't see. She could only hear the movement of carts from the hospital staff in the halls and smell the antiseptic scent that was so prevalent in hospitals at that time.

Suddenly, she could see again and found herself out of her body. In front of her was a school friend of hers named Jimmy. He asked her if she could walk him home which she was happy to do. They held hands and walked together toward the light and witnessed several spirits come through it. Ecstatic, Jimmy dashed toward them. He waved goodbye to Linda as his relatives embraced him, and they went into the light together. Linda then returned to her body. That night, unbeknownst to her at the time, Jimmy was taken to the same hospital as her after being in a car accident, passing away shortly thereafter.[4]

The notable thing about Linda is that in addition to this shared death experience, she also had two NDEs herself. You already read the first of them when she drowned at the age of four. The other was much later in 1986 after developing double pneumonia in a hospital. In both cases, she was told that there was more to learn before her time was up, but in the end, she had the final choice.

The last case I will mention is the one that really validates this phenomenon with 100 percent certainty in mind. In the first chapter, I briefly mentioned Scott Taylor's story where he witnessed seeing the spirit of his girlfriend and her son, who had just passed away in his hospital bed. The two had both been in the same car accident coming back from a trip to the lake, but it took the boy five days before he succumbed to his injuries. Because of that delay, dozens of family members heard about the accident and came to the boy's bedside when the doctors said it was time to say their final goodbyes.

Now since Scott was essentially just a friend of the family, he was in the back of the room sitting near the windowsill. While he was there looking at the boy in his final moments of life, he saw the boy's mother appear over the bed. Her spirit descended down to reunite with her son. Next, the spirit of her son turned and looked at Scott. Suddenly, Scott's consciousness leaped from his human body, and the three traveled to the light together before he was returned. When it was over, he actually had to cover his face because he was so overjoyed with the love he just felt that he could tell it would be very inappropriate for others to see him like that as they were still grieving.

It was much later in life that Scott found himself doing research on NDEs for a dissertation he was writing. It just so happened that a relative of his late girlfriend and son was one of the people he would soon be interviewing. He felt a little awkward meeting her out of fear that she might bring up the elephant in the room, but something incredible happened when he sat down to talk to her. She explained how she thought he was meeting with her to discuss what "they" saw that day in the hospital room. He looked perplexed and asked her what she meant. She then went on to describe having the exact same experience that he did. It turned out that she had also witnessed the mother embracing her son and going to the light with Scott. In fact, she had been right there beside them, meaning there were actually four of them who had traveled to the light together that day.[5] Thus, there were actually two healthy bystanders that witnessed the exact same phenomenon.

Is it possible for a person's consciousness to leave their body while they are still living? In this case, forces beyond their control orchestrated a way for that exact scenario to happen, allowing them a final chance to connect to their loved ones before they left Earth.

The modern term used for this concept is *astral projection*. It is the belief of some modern-day theorists that people can actually leave their human body and travel around as an astral body. It is in this form where our true selves exist. The roots of this belief actually date back to ancient times, occurring across many cultures.

I have known about this concept for a long time, long before ever hearing about NDEs. As a young boy, I thought it would be so cool to fly around in this way. However, I had only ever heard of it in connection with a person dreaming. Therefore, I figured that astral traveling was just a fantasy, part of a manifestation of our dreams. Then, one day something astonishing happened.

It was the first night after I started writing this book. I had woken up around two in the morning. As I opened my eyes, I saw my then six-year-old daughter sitting on the bed sheets on top of me. At first, I thought, "How did she sneak in here so quietly?" Her legs were crossed over each other above my waist, like a lotus position. Then, I noticed she wasn't actually sitting on the bed at all. She was floating about two or three inches above it! She just sat there, suspended in air with a smile on her face. After about five seconds, the image slowly faded.

I lay there in shock for several minutes, wondering what had just happened and what it meant. I got up to check on her in her room, and she was perfectly fine, sound asleep in her own bed. Was this a hallucination? I suppose, since spirits and the afterlife were fresh on my mind, it is possible. If so, it was a first for me. Perhaps I was seeing her astral body dropping by to pay me a visit? Your guess is as good as mine, but I like to think it was a sign that I was supposed to write this book—like she was smiling because she was proud of that decision.

CHAPTER FOUR

Family Reunions

So if there is an afterlife, who will be there to greet us on the other side? The idea of seeing old friends and family who have passed once more is a wonderful thought. What NDE-ers have revealed is that there are several spiritual beings who can greet us. While oftentimes they are family members, there have also been reports of seeing angels and religious figures, among others. For describing this array of spirit types, the term "light beings" or some variation of this is often used. In this chapter, we will focus mostly on the light beings who represent our relatives, while the more otherworldly beings will be discussed later on.

The fact that NDE-ers report seeing family members in such high numbers leads a lot of skeptics to conclude that these images must be emanating entirely from our own brains and causing us to see who we want to see. The truth is that which family members we actually encounter seems almost random, like seeing a great-grandmother instead of their own mother, for example. If one believes the images we see are generated from within us based on our own desires, then it seems rather odd that the souls that greet us are often distant relatives rather than ones we were closest to and loved the most here on Earth.

We see more than just our human companions, too. There are actually plenty of accounts claiming to have seen their old pets there. Some are from very early in their childhood, while others are more recent, and it seems like all the classic animal families are accounted for. There are cases involving dogs, cats, horses, and even birds.

What is truly fascinating about these light beings is that they appear in virtually all phases of the NDE. Some see their loved ones during their OBE right there in the hospital room, while some see them in the tunnel and others while in heaven. Some even see them here on Earth through their own eyes and in their dreams.

What typically happens is that soon after a cardiac arrest, and as the soul exits the body, NDE-ers are greeted by one or more spirits. They are often described as being in their prime, meaning they are the best versions of their physical selves (around age thirty).

In cases where the spirits encountered are much older relatives before the person's time, they are identified later only after viewing them in old family albums. Now, why should we be greeted by such an old relative? Are our closest loved ones busy living another life or existing in another realm? Are the spirits who welcome us our spirit guides or our guardian angels? A lot has been written about spirit guides. They are often thought of as light beings who are assigned to us to help facilitate our spiritual transition when the time comes. They may perform other tasks as well to help us achieve our goals here. While that is one possibility, they could also just be old spirit friends from our past lives, and perhaps together, we've been enjoying the journey of the human experience and waiting to greet each other after each trip before taking on our next adventure.

One case involved a truck driver named Brian Miller. He had a heart attack while on the road. He was rushed to the hospital, and after going into cardiac arrest, he moved toward the light, entered a beautiful garden, and walked along a pathway. Suddenly, a man and woman approached him. The woman grabbed his arm and explained that he shouldn't be there yet and that he had more to do at home. When he looked at the woman's face, he recognized her as his mother-in-law, who had just passed away about one week prior. She looked great and appeared to be at a much younger age than when he knew her. The man was his father-in-law, who had been gone for about seven years at that point. When he told his wife, it was, of course, reassuring to her that her parents were safe, happy, and together again.[1]

That story is actually quite unique in that the spirits he met were not blood relatives. The bloodline seems to play a huge part in the spirits that await us, as the majority of cases report seeing direct family relatives. There are even some cases where these relatives are accompanied by other light beings. While the person may not recognize them, they intuitively know them and feel like they have always known them. There are also quite a few cases involving children who, until then, were unaware that their parents had miscarriages before having them. It is only while in the NDE that they actually meet their brothers and sisters, who explain exactly who they are.

In one such story, a young boy named Colton Burpo suffered a cardiac arrest while in a hospital. While having his NDE, he met a female light being who claimed she was his sister and that she died in their mom's tummy. After returning to his body, he shared this information with his parents. When he told them this, his mother was in complete shock. She had miscarried before having her son and never spoke about it.[2]

These types of stories suggest that the soul exists before birth and inhabits the baby while still in the womb. This is a stunning revelation to consider, but also an important piece of the cosmic puzzle of how and why we came to be.

In another relatively famous case, a neurosurgeon named Dr. Eben Alexander had caught a life-threatening case of E. coli after a trip to Israel where he was conducting research. While in heaven, he rode on the wings of a butterfly with a beautiful girl. He was on one wing, and she was on the other, just smiling at him and assuring him that everything was going to be fine.

When he eventually recovered, he conducted research on his experience and his own life. He learned that he was actually adopted, and when he found out who his biological parents were, he learned he had a biological sister. She had passed away some years prior to this. The amazing thing was that his sister turned out to be that lovely girl on the butterfly wing.[3]

His story is well-known, in part because his profession and prior skepticism toward the afterlife, which gave his case more validity in the eyes of his scientific peers. Most neuropsychologists agree that heavenly experiences are manifested in the human brain as chemicals are released while the body is unconscious. To this, Dr. Alexander makes the valid point that because of the nature of his body's condition and the fact there was no brain activity at all during the time of his experience, it had to be real. The logical conclusion is that the soul remains conscious throughout whatever conditions the physical body is in.

Incidentally, the main chemical that some in the neuroscience community believe explains NDEs is called Dimethyltryptamine (DMT). It is a naturally occurring hallucinogen found in the body. The trouble with that theory is that while individuals who take this drug may indeed have incredible experiences, they are much more random than those found in NDEs. The types of experiences of an NDE can be counted on two hands. Every single person who has ever had one, regardless of language, religion, or culture, can link their experiences to the classic NDE paradigm. With DMT, there are no patterns like that. That is an important distinction to consider when evaluating the merits of that theory. Another key difference is the validity of the OBE reports. There have been some cases of people floating above their bodies during a DMT hallucination, yet it is only in NDEs where the person's claims are actually corroborated with remarkable accuracy.

Coming back to our examination of light beings, one strange observation is that just about all of the souls appear to be in the prime of their lives. Well, I guess that's not so strange. I mean, if you could choose your own appearance, would you want to appear old or young? Some Christians believe that we appear that age because that was the age Jesus was when he died and went to heaven. I think there may be another reason.

Isn't it also possible that, spiritually speaking, our appearance reflects the best version of our human selves? Here on Earth, we are flawed. Intrinsically, we know right from wrong and if we are on the right path, but we don't always choose that path? Why can't we always be at our best?

"Let your conscience be your guide." Perhaps that little cricket was onto something. Is our conscience more than just a voice in our heads? Is it our true self trying to guide the way? On Earth, we can strive for perfection, but of course, none of us gets there. Besides, didn't somebody once say that perfection is boring? It's the imperfections that make us human and give us wisdom (and make for good stories). We are led by human characteristics like ego, greed, and selfishness. It's in our very nature. In heaven, the soul is above all of that nonsense, and their appearance reflects that purity.

It should be noted that while rare, there are some reports of older and younger-looking beings, although regardless of their physical characteristics, they all seem to possess an ancient energy. For instance, children sometimes report seeing child-like spirits who may act as their guardian angels.

In 1982, at age seven, a young girl named Kristle Merzlock got to meet her guardian angel. Kristle had drowned in a friend's swimming pool and found herself in a black void, aka the waiting room. Soon, she was in a colorful tunnel with a bright, welcoming light at the end.

Then, a spiritual being appeared and approached her. She said her name was Elizabeth and claimed that she was her guardian angel. The being took her into the light to a bright garden-like environment with flowers, trees, and a stream. It was there that she met some of her old relatives and exchanged hugs. There were also two other spirits named Heather and Melissa that were strangers, but at the same time she felt they were old friends. They said that they were going to be born soon. Elizabeth said this was her last time being a guardian angel before she would be born into a human body. Eventually, Kristle was given a choice to return or stay, and she ultimately made a choice to return for her mother's sake.[4]

So what can we infer from her experience? Do we have

guardian angels who watch over us, protect us, and guide us to the next realm? How many close calls have you had in your life where you nearly avoided a collision with another car because you felt compelled to look up at just the right moment? It could also be that you missed an important appointment that made you upset at the time, but you didn't stop to think that maybe there was a reason for you to stay home that day. Maybe you just got super lucky.

When someone sees a spirit during an NDE, they often try to explain how they recognize them from their energy. Sometimes, they know someone is there beside them without even looking at them. Vision was part of their sensory perception in these cases, but there was something more happening. Nikola Tesla, the famous inventor and visionary, famously said very late in his life, "If you want to find the secrets to the universe, think in terms of energy, frequency, and vibration." I interpret that to mean that when broken down to its core, every form of matter that fundamentally exists can be defined as energy and measured in terms of its frequency and wavelengths. He is essentially just rephrasing Einstein's famous $E=mc^2$ formula into philosophical terms. That formula, by the way, may help explain the energy signatures perceived in NDEs.

As well-known as this formula is, have you ever actually sat down and thought about its significance? $E=mc^2$: Energy equals matter times the speed of light squared. It's saying that if a physical object were to travel at the speed of light, it would be converted to pure light energy. We know this to be true as all forms of energy on the electromagnetic spectrum travel at this speed (approximately 300,000 km/sec or 186,000 miles/sec). To put this formula in more practical terms, it is saying that matter and energy are equivalent to one another. It is just that they take different forms under certain conditions. If you heat up any physical object millions and millions of degrees, it is converted to its energy form.

So how much energy are we talking about? If you take something like a pineapple weighing about one kilogram and make it really hot, like hotter than our sun kind of hot, then the pineapple will release 9×10^{16} joules of energy, which is equivalent to about twenty-one megatons of TNT. That is a lot of energy! Now take that concept and apply it to humans. Consider the atoms that make up our bodies and our consciousness. Is it possible that part of our energy equivalent represents our spiritual form? Our wisdom, our understanding, our love, and perhaps even our personalities and humor? What do those things look like when visualized as light energy? One thing is for sure—their size would dwarf the insignificant bodies we think constitutes who we are.

CHAPTER FIVE

This Is Heaven

In one of Shakespeare's most famous soliloquies, he writes, "To die, to sleep. To sleep, perchance to dream; ay, there's the rub, for in this sleep of death what dreams may come...." This was Hamlet contemplating whether his actions on Earth would determine if his experience in the afterlife would be one of pleasure or pain. Growing up in late sixteenth-century England, Shakespeare would likely have been greatly influenced by the church and its teaching of heaven and hell. In this chapter, we will be exploring actual accounts of people who claim to have been there.

One of the most exciting parts of studying all of these NDEs is that you are able to actually paint a picture in your mind as to what heaven is like. Its description is the most consistent of all phases of the NDE. So far, we have explored what it feels like and some of the spirits who welcome us there, but what about the actual physical characteristics?

Betty Cone has made that trip. She had her heavenly experience while in a coma after being in a car accident when she was seventeen. She experienced more stages of the NDE than I am covering here since we are focusing only on the heavenly realm. Other aspects of her extended experience will be explored later.

After traveling through the tunnel, she described stepping into heaven as similar to stepping off of a space ship onto another planet. She said that heaven was an indescribably beautiful paradise, so the words she used to describe it are inadequate. Remember that "words put boundaries on things."

She said, "It's like everything breathes and vibrates with life." She described incredible flowers and landscapes with meadows and rolling hills. Even the grass was the most brilliant green imaginable and was perfect. It couldn't be damaged by stepping on it. There were colors that she hadn't seen before on Earth. She claimed that she could almost see faces on all the flowers as they swayed back and forth, and she could feel the love of God permeate from them. All around, she heard the sound of beautiful singing voices, performed by angels in perfect harmony. There was also a lovely fragrance that saturated all of heaven. Even to this day, she can still detect this aroma during moments when she feels closest to God. There was also a crystal clear, beautiful blue river. She could see all the way through it to the bottom. Like everything there, it seemed to have a gold sparkle to it.

She said there were walls surrounding the city in every direction. Plants and flowers seemed to be woven into the buildings and architecture, giving them the appearance of being alive. It was truly amazing.[1]

Her experience involved incredible stimuli that filled her senses. The one that stands out most to me is her description of the colors. They seemed much more vibrant, even unearthly. She and others claim they are almost cartoonish. One possibility I've considered is that they are perceiving colors at broader frequencies than our human eyes are capable of seeing. I'd like to talk a little bit more about the properties of light and how we interpret color to help understand this better.

On the electromagnetic spectrum, we can only see visible light, which is a range of wavelengths from about 380 to 750 nanometers. This accounts for less than 1 percent (about 0.0035) of the complete spectrum that exists, from radio waves to gamma rays. We have all heard that animals perceive the world differently than us. Just as birds have photoreceptors that allow them to see into the ultraviolet (UV) band of frequencies and reptiles can see heat through the infrared range, perhaps the eyes of our souls are capable of detecting energy at much broader levels. This might help to explain some of the unusual and vibrant colors in all of these heavenly observations. While birds can see UV light, ornithologists theorize that the purpose is to identify other birds, urine trails, and food sources. In all likelihood, they still see the same range of colors that we do; it is just that the things they see may have different colors associated with them and with better vibrancy. A good example of this is the iridescent feathers that peacocks and some other birds have. These special feathers refract light as shimmering colors as their angles change, and while they look cool to us, they must be absolutely stunning when seen with UV vision.

When light is picked up by our eye's retina, its photoreceptors generate electrical signals that travel to the brain where the colors get processed. These photoreceptors have millions of cones to help us do this, yet there are only three color types: red, green, and blue. All the other colors that we see require our brain to activate just the right balance of cones, resulting in our best guess at what each color should look like. There are even colors that we perceive which have no wavelength at all on the color spectrum, such as pink. Of course, we can still see what we think is pink through the brain's interpretation. Who's to say what true pink (or brown, magenta, sage, etc.) really looks like? It seems reasonable to assume that the eyes of our souls are programmed differently from our human eyes, just as different animals perceive light in their own ways.

The other thing that caught my attention was the way that flowers behaved, with each one being unique and alive. This suggests other factors that are influencing our perception. There is, in fact, another property of light that we can't see, but many other species can. It's called *Light Polarization*. Certain animals use it to navigate their world and locate food sources. To truly understand it, you have to understand how light waves behave. As light travels to the Earth from our sun, it has electric and magnetic fields, which each vibrate in different directions. Those vibrations are perpendicular to the direction the light wave is traveling. As light hits our atmosphere, it scatters in all directions as unpolarized light. When it hits the atoms of objects here on Earth, some of that light becomes polarized. I am sure you have experienced these effects when wearing polarized sunglasses where only some light waves carrying certain vibrations are able to pass through the polarization material.

Honeybees can actually see both UV light and the polarization patterns on plants to easily identify them. When we look at a field of yellow flowers, they can seem to blend together. Bees can identify each one individually, and because they process light so much faster than us (on the order of several hundred frames per second), they can do this while buzzing around in flight, detecting even the slightest movements. Their vision, along with a built-in solar compass, also allows them to know exactly where the sun is at all times, regardless of visibility.

I could go on and on about just how incredible the world looks to different animals (or sounds to them, as the same concept applies to sound waves that are beyond the limits of human hearing). I think the point is that there is so much more energy out there than we think there is. Perhaps our souls have sensory perception tuned to see this energy. There's also the possibility that this spectrum, large as it may be, represents only a portion of all the different forms of light. It's a continuum, after all, with infinite possibilities and we can only measure that which we know to exist in the natural world and in our known universe.

Let's look at another NDE from a man named Scott Drummond. In his case, Scott initially only shared his NDE with his immediate family and waited many decades before he shared it publically. I am so thankful to him for doing that as it was his story that sparked my spiritual awakening and was the catalyst that resulted in this book. I would like to share just part of his experience now.

After being taken to heaven by his spirit aide, Scott found himself standing in a beautiful field with his companion nearby. Just moments earlier, he had been watching a scene playout below him in an operating room, where his old body still remained. The two spirits had just journeyed to the light together and while he never looked directly at this spirit, he knew that it was an old and familiar friend.

While in heaven, he saw otherworldly trees with long trunks and leaves on top, and just to the right of them were miles and miles of gorgeous waist-high wildflowers. The colors were, in his words, "vivid and magnificent." Directly in front of him was a huge field of tall, vibrant green grass.

A cloudy, white mist appeared in front of him, and at this point, his spirit companion left. He felt completely at peace here. He suddenly was made to see his life review from birth until his death at twenty-eight. When it was over, he found himself wishing that he could have been a better person—someone who was less selfish and more devoted to his family. He felt compelled to walk forward toward the white cloud. An arm peeked through the mist. It was a big, strong arm that was visible from just below the shoulder onward. The hand was opened in a gesture suggesting Scott should hold it. He did so and was immediately told, "It is not yet your time. You have more things to do." The arm receded behind the cloud, and Scott was suddenly sent back to his body.[2]

While his story was deeply personal, it also contains classic NDE observations about heaven. The fields of flowers and trees are almost always reported in the exact same way. This particular vision of heaven transcends religious backgrounds, cultural upbringing, and country of origin. It is one of the great patterns of NDEs. So what does it mean?

Logically, you have to wonder why there are even wildflowers in heaven at all. The pretty, colorful flowers that we know today are the result of millions of years of evolution, mostly with the specific purpose of attracting pollinators, such as birds. It is something very specific to the ecosystem of Earth. Yet there they are in the afterlife. There is a possibility that while some refer to this place as heaven, that is only partly true. Flowers, trees, butterflies, and streams are things we humans recognize and appreciate on Earth. There is strong evidence this is a transitional place designed to help us acclimate to our new existence before moving onto higher spiritual realms.

One of the compelling arguments in support of this theory is that everyone reports this garden-like version of heaven in the same way. However, for some of them, they had never seen an environment like that before.

For example, there is case involving a twelve-year-old boy named Muktar who fell from a palm tree and experienced the same colorful, heavenly environment as described by countless others (e.g., tall green grass, mountain landscapes, and flowing streams). The thing is that Muktar is from a Muslim country where the only environment he had ever known was the sandy one of his village. The lush foliage he saw in his NDE would have been foreign to him, yet he clearly experienced it.[3]

To lend more credence to this theory, many near-death survivors actually see a boundary between this transitional realm and the higher dimensions. It is made clear to them that crossing that line means that they cannot return to their bodies. It's a point of no return once that action is taken.

One such case involves a woman named Karen. After dying in a car accident, Karen recalled being taken immediately to another realm that she described as the most beautiful place she had ever been. It was a park-like setting with many trees and a mountain landscape in the background with lots of flowers. The colors were vibrant and shimmery. Everything radiated with love and peace.

This description should start to sound very familiar by now. We could practically copy and paste it from one case to the next and it would still be accurate for each individual. What differs are the light beings that communicate with them.

In Karen's case, she was greeted by three spirit guides. One of them was her grandfather on her mother's side. Another was a spirit aide who led her from her human life to there. The third one was a female spirit that she felt was someone she knew from a previous life. She was told that once she had transitioned completely, she would know exactly who that third spirit was and meet many others.

She asked them if she could meet her paternal grandparents, as she was very close to them. The message she received was that they were in another level of heaven. She interpreted that to mean that they were in another solar system in a different galaxy. She was told that every level, including Earth, is connected to the spirit realms. Earth was the lowest level. The transition realm she was currently in was essentially just a loading dock. You had to pass through that area before going higher. The amount of learning she had acquired determined which level she would go to.

She also asked why she didn't remember the accident or actually dying. She was told that for her, it wasn't necessary to go through that death process, e.g., the outer body experience and the tunnel. It is better in some cases for the soul to be taken immediately to that realm. In her case, it was because of the nature of the accident.[4]

Her story certainly introduces some fascinating concepts, and in my opinion, perfectly illustrates why wildflowers are in heaven. This heaven is the gateway between our world and the spiritual realms. It would explain why the imagery we see there is so similar to the things we see here on Earth. It is all by design to give us a sense of familiarity before we move onto other realms. Even though people grow up in different environments, we are all programmed to appreciate these specific things from our planet. Getting access to the highest levels first means that we must learn certain lessons, kind of like prerequisite learning.

Within this heavenly realm, some have also witnessed what we would call universities with souls deep in study.[5] I'd like to believe that maybe they were planning their human lives and what they wanted to learn. In that sense, this transitional realm is almost like a travel hub with souls coming and going all the time. What an exciting place that would be!

Now, while the overwhelming majority of NDEs report having a wonderful and positive experience, there are some who claim something different. They say they went to hell. At first, I was reluctant to even study these interviews, as they contradict the fundamental truth drawn from all NDEs up to this point—a truth that says we all come from the same place of unconditional love and light and return there after this life. However, to ignore them would be selective bias, and in an effort to be objective, these cases were also investigated. Let me provide some examples.

I introduced Dr. Rajiv Parti earlier in the book regarding his OBE. He had what started out as a classic NDE. What happened after that was that he was sent to a hellish realm with lightning and thunder in which there were evil creatures with crooked teeth torturing him on a bed of nails! He recalled hearing the sound of many souls crying out. He came to the realization that he must have been a very selfish and uncaring person while on Earth. In his plight, he cried out for help, and the spirit of his father came and led him to a tunnel with a bright light. From there, he traveled to the light and was enveloped in love and acceptance, and he received his life review, a phase of the NDE that will be covered in great detail in the next chapter.[6]

Another case was reported by Howard Storm, who found himself being tortured and humiliated by many creatures, and he prayed to God to save him. He was rescued and the darkness turned into light. He was then comforted by several angels and shown his life review and the importance of love. Upon returning to his life, he quit his job and worked in a soup kitchen before attending and graduating from seminary school, becoming a religious convert.[7]

In another case, a young woman named Corynn Nutter detailed an experience that happened to her when she was just a preteen. She had drowned while playing in a hot tub at a friend's house after her hair got caught in the pump. After five days of being in a coma, she said there was a male spirit with red eyes, dark hair, and a beard standing in front of her hospital bed. He was very tall and started to approach her while holding a knife. To her left, there was a female spirit. She was a little girl about the same age as Corynn, with blonde hair and blue eyes, surrounded by a bright light. The beautiful spirit was smiling right at her. Suddenly, this loving spirit walked over to the dark spirit and grabbed his wrist, causing the knife to drop to the ground. His eyes turned blue, and he retreated out to a door made of light. Immediately after this, Corynn woke up from her coma and recovered.[8]

There is another theme in many of these hellish accounts. Early in their NDEs, there is often a recollection of seeing beings who resembled their loved ones. However, they were like pale versions of them, and the person can usually intuit that they are facsimiles. One of the people who had such an experience is Betty, whom you were introduced to earlier. After her spirit rose above her bed in her hospital room, she floated into the hallway and saw an old, feeble version of her grandfather with a group of other spiritual beings begging her to join them. She rejected their plea. Later on, she was able to meet with her real grandfather who looked fantastic. She was told that those other beings were essentially demons pretending to be her relatives.

These types of experiences may seem terrifying, but there is something else to note. The people who had them are just regular people with ordinary vices. They aren't ax murderers or drug dealers. Yes, they could have acted better. They could have been less selfish, but there are a great number of people who are incredibly selfish and they experienced positive NDEs in wonderful settings. The real silver lining is that they all eventually get saved by light beings. Some are relatives, some are religious figures, and some are guardian angels. Is this dark realm a manifestation of their own guilt as a way for their soul to understand that they must change the trajectory of their life? Are there both dark realms and ones of light, with our actions determining where we'll end up? There is evidence that supports both scenarios, but unconditional love is just that—unconditional. This suggests that if dark realms do exist, it is by choice that the soul would go there as self-punishment. What makes more sense is reconciling one's actions through karma.

CHAPTER SIX

Meeting God and the Life Review

The most extraordinary and pivotal moment of the NDE is when the person actually meets with God. Many describe feeling the presence of God's divine love, yet only some have actually seen him in a physical form. The visualization of God is often described as a bright, loving light, although some see him with more anthropomorphic characteristics. Those who do meet him often have their life review directly with him and discuss the most significant moments together. The communication is telepathic, just as it is with every light being. The delivery of each message is also immediately sent and received all at once. One term used to describe this form of information exchange is "superluminal telepathic communication."

Of all the phases, the life review is the most special, as it can actually occur at any point during the NDE. Some are shown their review by a light being, some are shown it by religious figures, like Jesus, some see it entirely within their own minds, and some, as I'll share, have it presented by God.

During a fatal car accident, Jeff Olsen was crippled and lost his wife and infant son. His oldest son survived. It was during Jeff's recovery that he had an experience that really changed his perspective on life and allowed him to be able to choose happiness over sorrow.

At this point, Jeff had been in the hospital for about five months and was having his last procedures done. Back at the scene of the accident, he had an NDE where he was able to connect with the spirit of his wife who tried to comfort him. He was about to have another profound experience. One night, he went into a deep, peaceful sleep and entered the same heavenly realm he had been to before. He described this realm as a place of "love and light" that he could only explain as "home." There, he felt no pain but only joy. He could walk and run, despite his leg being amputated and his other leg being crushed. He knew he was only in this special place temporarily.

He noticed a corridor close by and entered it. There at its end, he saw his youngest son, whom he hadn't seen since the accident, lying in a crib. He was sleeping as peacefully and beautifully as ever. He swept him up into his arms and described the interaction as "super-sensory." It felt more real there than here on Earth. He marveled at how his spirit was able to hold another spirit and feel it so tangibly. He was made to understand that all energy is tangible; there are just different levels and vibrations.

As he held his son so tightly, he felt an energy form come up behind him. The presence was incredibly powerful and full of cosmic knowledge, yet it was also so personal and loving. Just as his arms wrapped around his son, he felt arms wrap around him. It was at this time that he could feel a flood of knowledge download into his consciousness, and he felt his son meld into him as he melded into God. They became one.

During this poignant moment, he was suddenly made to experience his life. All of the moments were there—all the painful ones and all of the beautiful ones. It was made clear that even the moments where he felt that he had made the wrong decisions were just part of his learning. Everything would work out fine. He wasn't being judged for those decisions as there was only love and understanding. He now could see that his life was perfect exactly as it was.

Previously, he had believed that God had decided his life for him and the obstacles he faced were tests for him to prove himself. He could now see that it was actually himself, Jeff, who planned and created his own life. He decided the life experiences that would teach him what he needed to learn before returning home to the spiritual realms. The mistakes he made in life were irrelevant here. He felt complete and absolute unconditional love from God.

He provides a wonderful analogy to articulate this love. He recalled a moment while his son was alive when he was first learning to walk and how he would fall down, sometimes bumping into things or causing trouble. Yet, as a father, he would always love his son and probably chuckled when he made mistakes. He explained that is the same love God feels for all of us, only magnified to a level beyond our comprehension. As we struggle through life and start to grow, God is proud of us because we are his children, and we, too, are learning to walk.[1]

This story demonstrates just how much God can affect someone without saying a single word or even meeting him in a physical form. However, there are many accounts of people that do exactly that. In this first case, Jesus Christ is actually present during the person's experience. While spirituality has become a big part of my life, I am not religious. The only dogma that guides me is love, kindness and empathy. However, religion can influence who delivers information in NDEs and we will discuss its significance soon.

In this case, a twenty-six-year-old man died in a car accident and left his body. His spirit was suddenly observing the car from up in the air, where he could see it was enveloped in smoke. He floated down to the front of the car and saw his physical body. At that moment, he was sucked up into a tunnel, where he described it as almost like a roller coaster ride into heaven. It approached a white light ahead. As he entered it, an intense and loving presence surrounded him. He described this feeling like "Getting into a hot bathtub after being chilled to the bone in the cold."

In this white light, every question he ever had was answered immediately, like tapping into the universal database of knowledge. Soon, Jesus appeared and, with his right hand, gestured and said, "Come." The eyes of Jesus looked right into his heart in a loving gaze. His left hand was pointing, gesturing to look up. The man was still so focused on the beauty of Jesus that it took him a while to focus on where he was pointing. Jesus said lovingly, "Look." Up above was God in a seated position, waving with his right hand and patting his knee with the left one, gesturing to him to come forward.

The man was shocked that he would be worthy enough for God to want him. Then, he was suddenly on his lap. God was looking down upon him with a great smile. He felt safe and that he was finally home. When he looked down, he saw a photo album on the ground spread out with pictures of his life. When he looked at a picture, he was suddenly there in that scene, feeling and thinking exactly as he did the first time around, only this time he felt the feelings of others, too.

The first picture he looked at was an incident when he stole an item as a young child. When the moment was over, he was there looking at God. Obviously, there was no hiding from the fact God knew. When the man apologized for it, God explained that it wasn't a bad or good thing but simply a lesson for his learning. He saw another scene where he was teasing a girl in junior high because she was overweight and had a lisp; only now, he felt the pain he was inflicting on her. Again, God told him that it wasn't a bad or good thing because all of this was merely a lesson for his learning. Even in moments of heroism, like when he performed a great act by saving a woman's life, he was still told the same thing.[2]

This further demonstrates that our acts in this life are seen objectively by God and that the only judgment perceived is from ourselves, who are our harshest critics. There was also that access to spiritual knowledge, like he was part of a super consciousness. This is frequently observed in NDEs. Let's dive deeper into what exactly this knowledge consists of.

Trying to visualize this flood of knowledge probably conjures up scenes from *The Matrix*, where Neo learns Kung-Fu instantly by having the information uploaded right into his brain.[3] In reality, NDE-ers claim that they become one with the universe. They receive a complete understanding of every scientific law, and all of the questions they've ever had about the universe are answered! (I suppose that information might also include Kung-Fu.)

I imagine tapping into this information bank also grants us access to the collective knowledge of every life form that has ever existed (and perhaps ever will exist). I say this because all life reviews have one thing in common. Every single moment from our lives is captured. Every action we took, every thought we had, and every emotion we ever felt. The same is even true when we view our past lives. This tells us that the memories of souls from the past are also stored in this knowledge bank. Think about that for a second. Every moment of every human life, from our earliest ancestors through today and beyond, is available in this collective consciousness that we can tap into. This compendium of human experiences and universal knowledge is known in theosophy as the *Akashic records*.

The history nerd in me gets giddy just thinking about that. All of the mysteries of our world that scientists and archaeologists can only theorize about are suddenly revealed in every clear detail as if we somehow recovered some film archive of the ancient world and could watch these great moments in history. We could see the pyramids get built, learn about the people who constructed Stonehenge, or know what actually happened to the lost Roanoke Colony. Is there really any treasure on Oak Island? Did Amelia Earhart really go to the Marshall Islands? Okay, so these things are of little consequence in the grand scheme of things, but inquiring minds want to know! Well, guess what? We will all eventually know everything there is to know. Just be patient.

I want to share another account now involving a young woman named Erica McKenzie who experienced her NDE after her body finally shut down after taking diet pills for far too long. She recalled floating above her body and seeing the paramedics arrive on the scene. As soon as she internally told herself that it was time to let go, she was embraced by an incredible light and propelled through a tunnel with a tremendous force, quickly accelerating to the speed of light. This space was filled with a magnificent and familiar love. Eventually, she reached the end of the tunnel and was, in her words, "delivered into the hands of God."

She stood with God on her right and heaven behind them, looking into the universe at all of the galaxies and stars. Heaven felt like a planet to her. All of a sudden, she heard in her left ear the sound of a vintage movie projector, similar to one she experienced as a child in the town she grew up in. The stars in front of her then repositioned into the shape of a curtain that slowly opened up. Next, she heard, "Three, Two, One..." and the words, "The Life Review of Erica McKenzie," appeared on the screen. Her life review began to play out in front of her. It was just her and God in a movie theatre in the cosmos.

Her life review started from her birth and ended with her death. It focused on personal achievements and accolades from her life, such as awards she won in athletics and cheerleading. They were all happy events, and she was reliving them just like it was the first time.

When the movie ended, she was told telepathically to look down. There were some eyeglasses just in front of her. She was requested to put them on. Now, these glasses were huge, about the size of a vehicle, and she was wondering how she could ever put them on. In that very moment, her hands reached down, picked them up, and somehow, they miraculously fit perfectly. She was told to watch the movie again. Once more, she heard the countdown, and the movie played.

This time with God's eyeglasses, she could really see. Whereas before, she was seeing things that were important to her human ego, in this version, they were things that were important to her soul and to God. The scenes highlighted this time were moments where she showed love and compassion to those who needed it, the times she helped someone who was being picked on at school, or the times she gave money to a homeless person when she didn't really have money, even for herself. As she described it, every single action, word, thought, and feeling was about love. Just as in her first review, she was once again reliving these events. When the movie was over, she felt compelled to look up and, for the first time, saw God in a physical form. She could only see him from his shoulder down to his fingertips. In her estimation, his arm was bigger than a semi-truck. He raised his hand up, and it reached as high as the furthest stars. In the palm of his hand was a rock. With his arm expanded into the far depths of space, he suddenly released his grip and let the rock go. It fell for what seemed like almost an eternity. He told her, "You are the rock. You are the light." As he said the word "light," the rock lit up with an incredible brightness. It was almost blinding; it was so brilliant. Then, before her was a huge body of water that reached beyond her line of sight on all ends. The rock fell into this ocean of the stars, producing a single ripple. That ripple grew and grew until it was out of sight. God said to her, "You are the rock. You are the light. You are the ripple that affects mankind." It was then that she realized the significance of seeing two life reviews. Her purpose was far beyond being the person of Erica. It was about the positive influence on each and every person, some directly, but many indirectly.

Next, she was made to see huge, towering shelves all around her that seemed to reach out beyond the heavens. Each shelf had brilliant gifts. She was told that God gives everyone gifts and that they are all different. He stated that she was given the gift of patience and beauty. The patience to take time out of her day to help others and the beauty of the kindness in her heart. On Earth, her subtle actions could result in hugely impactful moments.[4]

I loved Erica's story both because of the message it inspires and also the beautiful picture it creates. I imagine a stone of light as a perfect metaphor for human beings and our potential. The stone represents our inner strength and convictions. The light emanating from it is our positive energy and the love we share. The image of this lighted stone falling on an endless ocean amongst the stars, producing a single ripple, would make a great painting... or book cover.

While some accounts describe God with human-like characteristics, there are also many who describe seeing him as a bright orb of light that transcends gender. In the first chapter, you read about one of those accounts. Another is that of Andy Petro. He was a senior in high school at the time of his experience and was at a class picnic when he drowned in a rafting accident. While at the bottom of the lake and stuck in the mud, he heard a voice telling him to rest and let go. As he did, he exited his body and instantly felt a wonderful sense of love and peace. After traveling through a tunnel, he collided with a giant ball of divine light, which he said was about the size of a basketball coliseum. He was suspended somewhere in the middle of it. In every direction, he saw "miniature motion pictures" of his life. He could sense every sensation and emotion that happened at that time. When he concentrated on one of the scenes, he was suddenly reliving it. After the life review was over, he popped out and was directly in front of this light. It was as bright as 10,000 suns, yet you could stare right into it.

He described the light as giving no judgment or shame, but only love and acceptance. The light started to speak to Andy within his mind, calmly saying, "Andy, don't be afraid. Andy, I love you. Andy, we love you." As God said that last sentence, suddenly billions of other lights lit up behind God. All of these light beings said in unison, "Welcome home, Andy."

Andy was then absorbed into this great light, and a massive download of information flowed into his consciousness. He suddenly knew everything about the Earth, nature, and the universe. The two laughed at some of the silliness of his life experiences on Earth and how he had taken things much too seriously. Andy said that God has a fantastic sense of humor.

Eventually, he was told that he had to go back.

Although he pleaded with God to let him stay, he was ultimately forced back into his body, which was now back on land. He was in tears, which his friends assumed was from the pain of drowning, but he was crying from all the love he had just felt.

Andy concluded his story by saying something incredibly profound and moving. He said, "Being in the light was being in unconditional love. Unconditional love means unconditional forgiveness. Unconditional forgiveness causes you to smile forever."[5]

Let's take that statement in for a moment. The concept that there is unconditional forgiveness implies that we can commit crimes without punishment. It's one thing to tease a kid in school or steal from a grocery store, but what about more serious crimes? What if you murdered someone? While it is true that in every life review, God doesn't judge them, he understands the judgment they put on themselves, reassuring them that it's okay. He plays the roles of a great teacher, a loving parent, a best friend, and a confidant, all wrapped in one.

During the life review, the spirit sees their words and actions in a way they could never understand in their human form. They often feel shame and guilt, and God will talk about this with them and discuss what was learned as a result. We haven't yet talked about reincarnation, but that is one possible outcome. Does the soul decide to live their next life as someone who will experience the suffering they inflicted on others, in a sense creating their own karma to establish cosmic balance? In Mahayana Buddhism, there is a concept that supports this idea called *Alaya Vijnana* (Sanskrit for "storehouse consciousness"). The belief is that this knowledge bank contains all of your experiences and impressions from previous lives, forming the seeds of future karma for you to endure in your current life.

There's another extraordinary thing that happens in some life reviews. While reliving the events, they will sometimes hear the spiritual voice of the people in the scene speak to them. I will admit, this part is a little spooky.

Remember Robert Bare from earlier? In his life review, he recalled the time when as a teenager, there was a girl that liked him and wanted him to take her to a local dance. At the time, he said that his car was his girlfriend—a 1957 Chevy that he often worked on. He declined to go and went out joy riding on the beach with his buddies. She was upset by this and wrote him a letter. That night she ended up going to the dance with three other people; however, on her way there, the vehicle was in an accident and she died. When his life review got to that point, he heard her voice say, "You never opened my letter!"

At a later point during that same life review, he was reliving a scene when as a highway patrolman, he was making an arrest during a riot, and he heard some gunshots and saw a man running toward him with a rifle. He told the man to stop, but he kept running. He could have lawfully fired at him but chose not to. At that moment in his life review, he heard the man's voice say, "Thanks for not shooting me."[6]

In another case, a man from Holland named Evert Ter Beek had passed away after having a heart attack and floated above the roof of the hospital where his body still remained. Next, he had his life review, and he saw an image of a young woman and an infant boy. They told him, "You abandoned us when we needed you the most." Now, the man didn't immediately recognize them, yet he felt he should. When he came back into his body and recovered, he was determined to find out who the woman was because she seemed familiar somehow. Eventually, he discovered it was a woman with whom he was romantically involved very early in his adult life. It turned out he fathered her son, who had died thirty years earlier. It was a powerful and difficult revelation for him to accept.[7]

In these examples, the souls who speak to us clearly relay a positive or negative response to the person's actions. While God may not judge, are these souls passing judgment or just showing human-like emotions? Or maybe these voices are how their human selves may have responded at the time, and we needed to hear them to grow and understand that our actions have consequences beyond our intentions, once again coming back to the ripple analogy.

Now let's just summarize some of these life reviews in terms of how they were presented. There was a movie theatre, a photo album, and some inside of God in the shape of an orb. There are many other types of settings reported, too, like seeing scattered pictures painted onto clouds, jumping into bubbles with scenes from their life, watching events on television sets, and viewing everything on panoramic viewing screens. So why are there so many unique ways that a life review can be presented, and why does God appear to different people in different forms?

At first, the skeptic in me didn't know what to make of all of this. Photo albums and television in heaven? These are modern human inventions specific to Earth! But what if they are just symbolic? God chooses the theme and presentation of each life review in a way that perhaps reflects the person's personality and memories, thus facilitating the delivery of this incredible information in the most effective way. Could we expand that premise to say that the religious figures so often reported are also selected for the same purpose? Does this explain why different people see different religious references?

CHAPTER SEVEN

Religion

In his iconic novel, *On the Road,* beatnik and poet Jack Kerouac wrote, "Tonight the stars'll be out and don't you know that God is Pooh Bear."[1] So did he literally mean that the creator of the universe is a stuffed bear with an addiction to honey? Maybe. It could also be that he meant religion is an invention to make us more comfortable. Knowing his penchant for alcohol, we can't rule out it was just the booze talking, either. However, there are some recent theories that actually use Winnie the Pooh as the embodiment of the Chinese philosophy of Taoism. (Yes, really!)

In Taoism, there is the principle of *pu* (pronounced just like the bear), which suggests we achieve happiness by seeing the world through a childlike simplicity, rather than overcomplicating our lives with constant analysis about why things are the way they are. It also states that everything has a purpose—human beings, birds, flowers, even Winnie the Poohs and Tiggers. So while Tiggers can't climb trees, Tigger thinks he can. In fact, that is what he believes he does best, even though he constantly requires Pooh to rescue him. That is his lesson to learn. When he discovers that his strengths lie with something else, he will have found his true purpose and be rewarded with inner peace.

Just about every major religion in the world aims for us to find inner peace through one path or another. Most also believe in the existence of an afterlife and that we have a soul. Judeo-Christians and Muslims believe our soul travels to another world where it spends eternity. Buddhists and Hindus believe in the reincarnation of the soul. While we have no written evidence for it, I would wager that the religions of our prehistoric ancestors also shared similar beliefs. There's another link between many different religions, including Judaism, Christianity, Islam, and certain Native American tribes—the concept of angels.

While we have described some types of spiritual beings, angels play a unique and important role in NDEs. Witnesses often describe them with striking similarity when asked about their physical appearance. They are often seen by young children during their NDEs, but they have also been reported by people of all ages in all regions of the globe. In the book *Closer to the Light,* Melvin Morse and Paul Perry interview many children who described them as ancient, otherworldly beings who are made of light energy. They stand between six and ten feet tall using Earth references. Their eyes appear to be made of pure light.[2]

In one case, a boy named Dean described his angel as about seven feet tall with bright, golden hair and wearing a long, white gown with a single belt tied at the waist. One researcher in the field named Dr. Craig Lundahl is a professor of Sociology who has written extensively on this subject. He found that angels seem to have three main functions during an NDE: to be a guide, a messenger, and an escort. The angel is often accompanied by other light beings who were deceased relatives of the person having the NDE.[3]

Another often-sighted biblical figure is Jesus. While many report seeing light beings in their NDEs, about 25 percent of them report seeing Jesus specifically.[4] He is usually described in terms of his energy rather than physical features. Witnesses report feeling his presence and how his love wrapped them like a blanket until they are simply overwhelmed by it. They feel totally accepted by him through his unconditional love and absolute forgiveness. Those who have seen him in a physical form describe him in different ways.

Some see him as a dark-skinned man reminiscent of what someone would have looked like who came from the Middle East. Others see him with lighter skin, like his depiction on the many renaissance paintings throughout Europe. Some see him in a plain robe, while others see him as a well-dressed king.

Well, this seems rather strange. If Jesus did once exist as a human being, he would have appeared to people in the same way, likely as a brown-skinned man with an ordinary tunic and leather sandals. In his 1973 speech in South Africa, Reverend Billy Graham described him with similar logic, saying, "He came from that part of the world that touches Africa, and Asia, and Europe, and he probably had a brown skin." He continued, "Christ belongs to all people. He belongs to the whole world."[5]

So in life, he appeared as just a man who looked like other ordinary men of his time and culture, but to us, he appears in unique and special ways. Just like God and the life review also differ in their presentations, perhaps he appears in a way that will make the strongest connection to us spiritually.

Not to get too off-topic, but this same logic could also apply to how we recognize other souls in the spiritual world. For example, your soul's physical appearance would resemble the way you looked in life when seen by your loved ones, so they can easily recognize you when they pass. Hypothetically, if you were reincarnated before they had a chance to reunite with you, then would you still appear to them as you did in that life or would you look like the person from your most recent human incarnation? It seems logical that if both of your families from each of your previous lives were to see you in heaven, then you would appear to each of them in a unique and recognizable way. Our souls likely have particular energy signatures that transcend how we looked physically. In NDEs, we see other souls with human characteristics because that is how our consciousness interprets their energy in a way for us to easily recognize them.

So how does religion fit in to all of this? To help better understand that, let's explore some examples of the experiences people have with religious figures.

In the chapter on heaven, I shared a portion of Betty's fantastic NDE. I'd like to discuss how religion played into her experience while she was in her coma. While in heaven, she was immediately welcomed by her grandfather, appearing in his prime. He explained that he was there to greet her. Like in all NDEs, the communication was telepathic. They spoke for a little while, and then a huge crowd of spirits came up to her. She sensed that each one of them was a past relative, some she recognized and others she didn't, yet it was clear that they all knew her. They all looked great and at the best point in their lives.

Then another man approached her, who she says was Abraham, the father of the faith from The Bible. He wanted to reassure her that she'd be fine and that he was going to give her a tour. Heaven was a beautiful paradise, much like the other examples you read about earlier.

She noticed a gathering of spirits getting excited while looking over to the hills beyond the city gates. It was on these hills in the distance where a bright ball of light could be seen. She says it was like the sun had sat down on the Earth and was moving across the field. This bright star slowly made its way closer to her until she could see that there was a person inside of it. Soon enough, she could see that it was Jesus and that the ball of light was from the light beaming off of him. Even from where she stood, she could feel the love radiate from him. Abraham explained that it was time for the two of them to meet. They floated up the field toward him, but she became weak. She felt that she wasn't spiritually strong enough to see him. Abraham then led her to some fruit trees along the river. She was told to pick one of the fruits and eat it. At first, when she tried to grab one, she lost her grip, and it fell. She was still learning how to interact within the spiritual environment she was in. The fruit simply evaporated on the ground, and a new one appeared in the exact spot where she had grabbed the first one. She was told there are no mistakes in heaven. Everything is perfect. This time she grabbed it and put it toward her mouth, where she absorbed its energy. It was extremely satisfying. She then felt the inner strength to continue moving. It was then that she met with Jesus.

While at first she felt vulnerable and exposed because he knew everything about her, his love and kindness were so overpowering that she felt completely comfortable. He explained that she still had more to do and had to return. She was hesitant to do that, insisting that she stay. So he let her feel the prayers from Earth from those she left behind. She could see an image of her mother crying and praying for her. She suddenly became part of her own funeral, and, rising above her casket, she saw and felt everyone around her before she was brought back before Jesus. He reminded her that while she had the final choice, it was best for her to return and fulfill her purpose. She was told that if she chose to remain in this spiritual realm, then she would be "over there." As he said that, he raised his arm and pointed to what looked like outer space. She took this to mean that it wasn't hell but rather a different realm from where she currently was at. Access to the higher dimensions would only be granted to her if she returned to Earth to complete her obligations there. She then agreed, and his face lit up with the brightest smile. He reassured her that they would see each other again one day.[6]

Clearly, this person had a very personal experience with an energy form she believes was Jesus. She had his undivided attention, and that is true of all spiritual encounters with him. If Jesus is real and came here to Earth, you could just imagine the lines of people waiting to meet him. We'd have to take a number and wait our turn, like at the DMV, only magnified times a million. Yet in your spiritual form, he is there only for you for as long as you both need—just one of the amazing perks of timelessness.

Now you might assume that those who report seeing Jesus were predominately Christians, and you'd be right. So it makes sense that they would see him. While there are also some agnostics who meet him, even they are often brought up with Jesus as a sort of symbol of heaven, so the subconscious connection is still there. With a few exceptions, Jesus does not appear to people who were not exposed to any form of Christianity whatsoever.

So we keep mentioning Jesus, but what about people who follow other religions? Do Buddhists see Buddha? Do Indians see their Gods? Do Muslims see Allah? (Did Kerouac see Pooh Bear?) I will admit that most of my studies come from North America and Western Europe, which is predominantly Christian, so the religious figures present mostly stem from The Bible. However, there are several research papers and other case studies that involved Hindus, Jews, and Muslims that had fascinating results. I've already shared some findings from near-death survivors brought up with Hinduism, such as Jang Jaswal and Dr. Rajiv Parti. While neither saw Hindu Gods or other religious symbolism from their upbringing, they both did have many elements of the NDE patterns. They both met with light beings who helped them to see their true purpose, and they both described the golden white light shining on them. Dr. Parti actually met with two guardian angels named Michael and Rafael. Incidentally, his wife teased him about seeing angels with Christian names by asking, "What happened to the thousands of Hindu Gods!" Dr. Parti theorizes that because he has lived in the US for so long, it's possible some western symbolism might have influenced what he experienced. Since this is such a small sample of cases, I'm hesitant to draw any conclusions, but they do offer interesting insights.[7,8]

Now let me share the results of a study done on Iranian Muslim NDE survivors. In 2020, the results of a joint study performed by multiple universities in southeast Iran were released. Of the surviving patients, eight were interviewed who had NDEs. All the patients reported having extremely pleasant experiences. Three of them reported the tunnel phase and traveling toward an increasingly bright light. One of their descriptions was translated to say, "When I was in the CPR room, I just remember I was going through a tunnel. Of course, I did not go myself. I was carried by others, and at this moment, a light blocked my path." I interpret that to mean that his soul was being carried by angels or spirit guides through a tunnel with a great light at the end.

Two of them had outer body experiences and saw the medical personnel work to revive them. One of them had a life review, and one heard his deceased uncle reciting words from the Qur'an.[9]

These reported sensations are the same classic NDE phases described across all cultures. The particular sensation of hearing spirits referencing religious texts extends to other religions, too. There are also accounts where the specific religion the individual practices plays an even bigger part in the NDE.

A spiritual counselor named Nomi Freeman shared one such story that her rabbi friend had told her. The rabbi was teaching a Torah class in Israel and was approached by an elderly woman who asked if they could offer Torah classes in English because of the growing number of English-speaking people living in Israel. She volunteered to teach them, and it soon became quite popular, with many friendships formed out of it. However, the woman was growing quite old and had to retire after just a couple of years of teaching the class. She moved in with her son in his house.

Two years later, the rabbi received a call from the woman's son. He was told she had been unconscious for several days, but upon waking, the first thing she asked, with much joy and excitement, was to please call the rabbi. The son asked if the rabbi could travel to see her as she didn't have much longer to live. He agreed, cleared his schedule for the rest of the day, and immediately drove to the hospital.

The woman told the rabbi that while unconscious, she went to the other side. There were spiritual beings there who showed her a gift that was meant for her, explaining that she would be traveling to this place soon. The gift was a crown made from her good deeds. The centerpiece jewel of that crown was the Monday night Torah class she taught. She pleaded with the rabbi to continue the class, which of course, he did. She passed away later that same day.[10]

In her case, the woman was told that her teaching of Jewish scripture was her biggest accomplishment in life.

However, there is another way to view this. It's possible that her centerpiece jewel had more to do with bringing together people who may have felt isolated before and helping them discover who they are as opposed to the scripture itself. Perhaps it isn't the religion that is the most important thing, but rather choosing the one that helps you to discover your best self and true destiny. Recall how many NDE-ers are told that the pathway to heaven transcends religion and that each religion can be helpful in reaching your soul's potential on Earth. Consider Howard's experience from earlier in the book. Before returning to his body, he asked what the best religion was. The answer he was given was, "The one that brings you closest to God."

It is not just religious practitioners who see religious figures. Randy Kay was agnostic and had a religious NDE. It happened during a cardiac arrest, stemming from a severe blood clot that he likened to a traffic jam in his whole body.

He recalled rising high above his body into a lighted area. He could see some spiritual beings in the distance. Then he felt a soft body next to his. This being was soon cheek-to-cheek with him. Randy felt a comfort he had never felt before. He thought, "So this is love..." During this sweet gesture, he slowly turned to see who this spirit was. He recognized him with total certainty as Jesus. He was emanating with love. For a while, they just remained there in silence and complete peace. To him, he felt like he was an audience of one and that all of this divine attention was just for him. He referenced a passage from the Bible to articulate this feeling of divine love:

John 4:7 "Beloved, let us love one another, for love is of God; and everyone who loves is born of God and knows God."

He was eventually returned to his body, after which he

converted to Christianity.[11]

So the question that is top of mind for most is whether this is really Jesus interacting with all these near-death survivors, or is the image of Jesus being portrayed by God because it was what these souls needed to experience at that moment to realign themselves with their top priorities? There are just so many cases like this one that it's hard to dismiss them all. In fairness, the vast majority of them involved people who grew up with Christian symbolism in their lives. We have only a relatively small sample of NDEs from other cultures where that is not the case. While there have been attempts to solicit more NDE research from other religions and regions, they just don't report as many as in the West. However, there is a logical explanation for this. Other cultures are more reserved than the uninhibited Westerners. Those other cultures likely have the same incidence of NDEs, but they just choose to keep them private. In fact, many in the West do the same, viewing it as a sacred and personal event.

So from the cases that we do have, what is the final conclusion to draw from the role of religion? As mentioned earlier, I feel that religion can and does help many people realize their full potential. When we look at all of these NDEs, I tend to focus more on the message than the messenger as the true kernel of truth. Religious figures help facilitate the transfer of cosmic knowledge and understanding in a way our minds can process. Some receive this from other spiritual beings, some get it from God, and some find it from within themselves.

The final case I will share before concluding this chapter incorporates religion, but more importantly, it creates an image and a universal truth that I feel is at the heart of all NDEs. In this account, a woman named Theresa had passed away in a hospital due to her body's reaction to some drugs that were given to her there. Her voyage to heaven included the archetypal tunnel and light, along with overwhelming love, access to divine knowledge, and deep intuition that she was safe.

Upon her arrival in heaven, she was greeted by a male spirit dressed in a robe. She saw a large table with thousands of spirits communicating with each other. They were laughing and having a good time. Suddenly, one of the spirits rose up and looked right at her. It was her grandmother. She told her, "It is not your time yet." To this, Theresa replied, "I am staying. I love it here. I am accepted here for what I am."

Then, she saw in the other direction another much smaller table with just two light beings. She was told by her spirit guide that one was an angel, and the other was a spirit who had committed suicide and was being encouraged to remain there.

Next, she asked the spirit to her side if she could see Jesus, whom she called "The Christ." In that moment, another presence appeared on her other side. Sure enough, it was Jesus. She looked up at his face. She described him as being made of brilliant light. She was drawn to look at him and felt totally accepted.

Very soon after, she had her life review. She could see a screen with all of the faces of the people she had interacted with during her life. She felt the intensity of the emotions that each of them felt, whether it was a positive or negative moment. It happened very fast. She was then asked by Jesus what she had learned from seeing these faces. She replied, "Love was the best choice." He agreed and told her that we must be careful how we treat people.

Next, she was taken to a pond. Jesus dropped a stone into it. He explained, "Your actions are just like the ripple effect in that pond. Everything you do not only affects those people, but it affects those that ripple on and further out." She is then instructed to return to Earth. Before she left, Jesus told her to remember three things to take with her. Number one was to show more love. Number two was not to be afraid of what you leave behind. The third and final instruction was to just enjoy life.[12]

Now you should recall that this same ripple in the water analogy was also presented to Erica in the previous chapter. It's actually a very common scene viewed in NDEs. How strange and incredible for so many different people from different backgrounds to see the exact same analogy demonstrated. The concept of our words and actions rippling through many lives is an old one. It has been a staple principle taught by teachers of Zen Buddhism for many years. I can recall one parable where a wise, old Buddhist master is explaining the concept to one of his students. He drops a stone in a pond and asks the student to stop the ripple. The student reaches down as the ripple approaches him and puts in his open hand to stop it. When his hand touches the water, it only causes more ripples to develop. The master explains that it is important to think before we act, for once we have acted, the ripple is beyond our control.

The idea has also been used often in the stories we hear. An early example can be seen clearly in *It's a Wonderful Life*. As a kid, I even remember it being a common theme in one of my favorite science fiction shows, *Quantum Leap*.

In practically all NDEs, God (or whoever is conducting the life review) always reiterates that life is about learning. Some moments are big learning events, and others are small ones, but they all shape who you are and affect others in ways you never imagined.

CHAPTER EIGHT

The Seeds of Time

When I was younger, I used to think about astronauts one day installing huge mirrors on the moon. These would be the biggest mirrors ever made, perhaps even miles across. So why did I want to do such a silly thing? One reason—to travel through time!

As most of us know, when we look at the stars in the night sky, we are seeing the past, light that took hundreds or sometimes thousands of years to reach us. The same principle applies to nearby objects like the moon. Even when looking at yourself in the mirror just a few feet away, you are technically seeing a past version of yourself. The light from the moon takes about 1.3 seconds to reach us. If you had a powerful enough telescope, and you looked at a giant mirror on the moon reflecting back on you, then you would be looking at yourself from 2.6 seconds ago. If you put two giant mirrors on the moon and one near your location on Earth at just the right reflective angles, then you would see yourself from 5.2 seconds ago. With enough mirrors and if perfectly executed (and calibrated to account for Earth's rotation), you could even see several minutes ago. You might even disappear from view completely because you'd be looking at the spot where you were standing before you had gone outside with your telescope and stood there. Time is a funny thing, isn't it?

I thought, with enough mirrors, I could see back hundreds of years and watch history play out for my amusement (with weather permitting, of course), and there's a lot of history to be seen. Thinking back now, I can see that there are a lot more variables to consider, but it was the fantasy of a little kid, so we can forgive the oversights.

The moon has been around for almost the same amount of time as Earth, watching over us for some 4.5 billion years and counting. It has seen us survive multiple ice ages. It has seen civilizations come and go. Leveraging it is one extreme (and somewhat crazy), theoretical way we can look back in time at Earth's past, but what about seeing the future? Is it possible? A lot of people seem to want it to be. There's certainly no shortage of science fiction literature written on this topic.

One of the all-time classic stories about this is Shakespeare's *Macbeth*, where the title character is told his fate by three witches known as the weird sisters. He is told that he will become the new king of Scotland. Then his best friend, Banquo, inquires about his own future, discovering that he will be the father to a line of kings. Both men are baffled by the news, but naturally, all of the predictions come true as Macbeth murders King Duncan, ascends to the throne, then kills Banquo in an effort to ensure only his line survives. Meanwhile, Banquo's son escapes capture and goes on to father future generations of kings. The real question for me is whether this prophecy would still have come true if the two men had not met the witches and been told about everything in the first place? Did the predictions come true, in part, because the protagonist wanted them to, like a self-fulfilling prophecy? It's one of those crazy paradoxes that is fun to debate with friends but seemingly impossible to answer.

One of the remarkable revelations of NDEs is that we are able to see both our past and future. In fact, we are made to understand that we were the ones who chose this life. We helped plan out the lessons that we should learn and the people who could help teach them to us. This includes specific events and milestones and when they should happen. We even selected the environment we'd grow up in and the families that raise us. (So we can stop saying that we don't choose our parents. We do!) This means that our soul has, in many ways, chosen our human destiny for us before we even take our first breath. The question is, how do we rediscover that destiny so that we can successfully fulfill it?

The environment in which we can see our future is usually the spiritual realm of the NDE, but they can also happen in our dreams or even by loved ones while fully conscious. There are even special cases of people who got to see and meet their future children, who selected them to be their parents. Let's look at examples from each of the different delivery modes.

Circling back to Robert's case, just a couple of weeks before his NDE, he woke up in the middle of the night and saw his deceased friend in spirit form standing at his bedside. He appeared much younger than he was when he passed away. He told Robert that he would be taking him to the light soon and to get ready. He then told him that he had to leave to see his grandkids in Sacramento. (It was later confirmed that the friend's grandkids did indeed live there). Robert collapsed later that month while boarding a plane and was escorted to the light by the spirit of his friend.[1]

In this case, the encounter with the spirit took place while the person was alive and awake. Does this suggest that spirits can take the form of ghosts who appear in our physical realm? What exactly is a ghost, anyway?

Well, when someone asks you, "Do you believe in ghosts?" you should probably get clarity about what they mean. Are they referring to spirits who descend from another dimension to visit or escort a loved one to the light, or do they mean a ghost in a haunted house that chooses to stay on Earth? For me, the former is a possibility, but I am a bit more skeptical about the thought of spirits choosing to just hang around on Earth. The reason is because after we die, we can float around in spirit form for a little while, but sooner or later, we get sucked up into that proverbial tunnel. In other words, we don't have a choice as to whether our spirit form remains here or moves on. It is beyond our control. So while I love the movie *Ghost*, Sam running around New York City until he decides to enter heaven is just pure fiction, in my opinion. Still, I will say that the ending scene where his soul is received and greeted is actually a somewhat accurate depiction of what can happen based on the accounts given.[2]

Let's move on to another type of precognitive experience that takes place in an NDE. One case of this kind involves Dr. Mary Neal, who at the time of her accident was a full-time surgeon and director of spine surgery, and the mother of four young children. During her NDE, she had a life review and met spirits who she intuitively knew had loved and known her for as long as she has existed. She was in a peaceful place with flowers that emitted a wonderful aroma. She was told it was not her time, and she had to return. She was made to know the challenges that would be ahead as learning experiences that she had to face. It was there that she was told that her oldest son would be killed in an accident. She asked why and was returned to the part of her life review that explained that "beauty comes of all things." About ten years later, her son died in that car accident.[3]

While that event is unquestionably tragic, you have to wonder if Mary and her son planned for that to happen as part of the experiences that Mary needed in order to grow spiritually. It makes you wonder how many accidents are planned versus purely accidental?

Finally, let's look at the last method by which one can discover their future. That would be the visions seen in dreams. Earlier, I introduced Karen, who spoke about her heavenly experience and the different dimensions of existence. There was more to her story than just that part of her NDE. Several months before that event, she had a vivid dream in which she was in a car accident and died. She remembered every detail of the event, including the fact that the vehicle that hit her had been a utility truck that had run a red light. She even recalled the name of the company written on the truck. Well, for close to a year, she was constantly on the lookout for that truck and was a nervous wreck every time she had to drive. Her parents told her it was just a dream and to move on. Eventually, she let it go. She didn't want to live the rest of her life in fear. Just a few days after making that decision, she was blindsided on an onramp by the exact same truck from her dream.

During her NDE, she was given her life review with a focus on the lessons learned. Karen was still deeply connected to her young son and husband that she had left behind. The spiritual beings explained that those feelings were the human side of her clinging on and that things would be okay. She was made to see what happened next in the future if she remained in the spirit realm. She saw that her husband would eventually remarry a blonde woman that she described as "pretty and very sweet." She felt comforted by knowing he would find happiness again. She saw that her grandmother would help get her mother through her untimely death. She was also made to see that she would still be able to connect to them in a spiritual way. What ultimately made her decide to return was that she saw that eventually, her husband and the new wife would have their own child and that her son would be treated differently as a result. She wanted to make sure her son got as much love and attention as she would have provided, and so she returned.[4]

Karen's story is interesting in that she actually had two different forms of future visions. First, there was the dream, and then the scenes projected by the spirits in her NDE. There were two possible futures that hinged on her decision to stay or return to her body. Incidentally, most are forced to come back to their human body to complete their learning, but those that do get the choice are often shown how things will play out if they stay in heaven. Perhaps the vision of her death from her dream was the original plan, but because there was more to do and learn after the accident, she was offered a chance to return to further enrich her soul.

There are more accounts of connecting to the spiritual world through our dreams than you might expect. Our dreams play such a significant role in our lives, yet we still know so little about them. Yes, from a biological perspective, they regulate our metabolism and maintain the health of our brain and body, but what about their spiritual purpose and meaning? Much has been written on this topic, including psychoanalyst Sigmund Freud, who wrote probably the most well-known book of them all called *The Interpretation of Dreams* all the way back in 1899.

My own belief is that dreams are often fragments of memories and other sources that get stitched together as a coherent (or sometimes incoherent) storyline. Sometimes deep-seated fears and desires are interwoven into scenes that play out like a film. We often see faces from the past, and sometimes we meet new ones (or perhaps they're ancient ones from before this life). Sometimes the people in our dreams are friends and family, yet they look different from how we know them. Is our brain mismatching our memories, or are we seeing them as they once were in a past life?

There are so many different sources that help construct our dreams that it can be hard to draw meaning from them if there is any meaning at all. However, for some, the underlying message can appear crystal clear and is delivered by the spirit of a close friend or family member. There are theories that dreams may serve as a conduit for spirits to communicate with us. A link between two different planes of existence. Often, after the death of a loved one, their spirit appears in our dreams to let us know they are going home. They offer comfort and guidance when we need it the most.

Paul McCartney had such a dream in 1968 at age twenty-six, which inspired one of his songs. During that time, he was in a difficult period in his life, and one night, he had a dream where he was visited by his mother, who had died when he was just fourteen. He recalled seeing her face so clearly, especially the detail of her eyes. She told him in a reassuring voice, "It's going to be okay. Just let it be." We all know the classic song that resulted from that dream.[5]

Sometimes the dreams come from the person who is about to die to provide a preview of heaven. An elderly woman named Leah had a dream in which she was in another world where she walked through beautiful rooms with spiritual beings. Leah was told that she had accomplished what she needed to do in this life and would soon be coming home to this place. The woman was scared to tell her children for fear they would be frightened, but she did tell one close friend of hers who shared that account with them after the woman passed away later that year.[6]

During the NDE, there can also be an extremely

fascinating event that happens to just a small percentage of near-death survivors. They are actually able to meet their future unborn children in their NDE. The aforementioned Dr. Lundahl collected and researched many of these special cases.

In one of them, a man named Calvin saw a group of young children playing together in his afterlife experience. Calvin claimed that his eyes were fastened upon one of the children, and a message was instantly impressed in his mind that this little boy would be his future son. Sure enough, he became the father to this child soon afterwards.

In another fascinating case, Dr. Lundahl learned about a woman named Bertha who had become seriously ill and lost consciousness. She found herself above her body, looking down and seeing her nurse next to it. She met a female spirit guide who took her to the heavenly realm where she was brought to a large room and met with several former friends and loved ones.

The guide then took her to another room where there were many small children present. On the far side of the room, she focused on two little girls who were strangers to her, but were so beautiful that her eyes connected only on them. The guide explained that those girls were to be her next two children.

Bertha soon recovered, and she ended up giving birth to those two girls just one and two years later, respectively.[7]

So if we are to accept these experiences as truthful, it begs the question as to where the line gets drawn between free will and predetermined fate. Do we have any influence at all to the course of our lives?

There have been a lot of studies in neuroscience lately

devoted to free will. With brain monitoring methods, such as electroencephalography, we can actually see a ramping up of brain activity just before the conscious thought is conceived and the relevant action is performed. Things like eating food, playing the piano, or even the formation of the words you were about to say before you even thought to say them. Something in the unconscious mind that scientists are still trying to understand may be responsible for almost everything we do, effectively suggesting that our ability to make conscious choices is an illusion.

The extent of that influence is debatable, but both spiritualists and even the most devout religious circles agree that free will and predetermination both play some role as active ingredients in the makeup of our lives.

Take for example evangelist Billy Graham, who spoke about these concepts while promoting his book, *Facing Death and The Life After*. During a 1988 interview with Larry King, he explained that there is a time to be born and a time to die and that those exact moments are planned ahead. He referenced a seventeenth-century theologian named John Trapp while confessing, "If I had a time to die, then I would want to die the exact moment God wants me to die."[8] Now Billy Graham believed it was God who was orchestrating all of our life events, whereas many NDE-ers believe it is us with the assistance of God. Regardless of who planned it, we appear to be living out a story that has already been written.

Dr. Moody made an observation that further confirms this. While working in geriatrics, he noted that many of the elderly people he spoke to felt that as they grew older, they got the sense that their lives were like a script and they were just playing a part. Dr. Moody admits that even he experiences this intuition sometimes.[9] I have to confess that I too have had moments of *déjà vu* for things that should have been firsts for me. Perhaps all the world's a stage after all.

Even with that all being said, I believe there is free will and our decisions matter. Maybe the big milestones and intersections of our lives are planned, but what about everything in between? In the ripple analogy that God demonstrated for Erica, he said this of free will: "You get to choose if you let your light shine or not, but you are going to make a ripple."[10]

We have the choice to make good or bad decisions. Our actions can be motivated by love or hate. Whether we know it or not, the things we do and say influence the actions of others. So while some of the events in our lives may be predestined, we still choose how we react to them. We can choose how to treat one another. We can decide to show kindness, even when it is easier not to. By letting your light shine, your ripple brings light to the lives of others. Our field of influence far exceeds our field of view, and the consequences of our choices often apply to people we've never even met, along with those closest to us.

Each of the choices we make in every moment of every day can be seen as distinct waves in an ocean of possibilities. Some waves are formed out of fear and will spread fear wherever they go. Others are made out of love will carry that influence with them. Our free will to be kind and make good choices allows us to drift or align in the path that leads to our God-given potential. The ego in us thinks reaching our potential requires us to influence the world in some big way through a giant tsunami, but it's all about the little waves we make, letting our ripple do the rest.

Think about the last time you were running late while driving your car, and someone was trying to merge into your lane. Do you let them? Well, if you were in their exact position earlier that day and the drivers were being jerks and not letting you in, then you might feel like acting like a jerk to this driver. Why should you pay a stranger any favors when they don't pay you any? But if a driver was kind and had let you in, then you might feel like applying the same courtesy to them. This reciprocal behavior is what we call "paying it forward." So when someone helps you out of a jam, you are more likely to help the next person.

I recall a situation from several years ago while at a crowded holiday event downtown. Now, large crowds downtown tend to attract meter maids who are on the hunt for their next victims. I was still having fun at this event, totally unaware my meter was about to expire, and it would have, except some good Samaritan had put some coins in it for me. They left a note saying that they saw the situation, decided to help, and all they asked in return is for me to help the next guy who needed it. This was such a simple gesture, but it totally made my day. So it doesn't have to be some crazy act of heroism. It can be simple things like that that inspires us to be better human beings.

When we go off-script by deviating from the path intended by our soul, it can lead to accidents or early death. This may be why we are so often told, "It is not yet your time." We had planned to touch more lives and experience more lessons before our time was through. What is also clear is that committing suicide is certainly never part of that plan, nor is being the victim of murder. In fact, the effects of these violent deaths seem to linger into our next lives, requiring us to reconcile them by cosmically balancing those events to cultivate our spiritual growth.

There is another element to recognize as well—the concept of time. In our empirical universe, space and time must both exist together for us to perceive reality in the way we do. This space-time continuum allows us to perform everyday tasks and interact with each other. If you tell your friend that you want to meet for lunch, you must first ascertain when before you can do so, otherwise the two of you might go there at different times or even on different days. To meet each other, you must be at the exact same location at the same time.

However, our souls may be from a dimension without time. If that is true, then we could communicate and interact with anyone whenever we wanted. If we can accept that premise, then the events that to us on Earth are in the future, are to the spirits events that already happened. They get the privilege of seeing our lives unfold before we even experience them. Sometimes, they feel compelled to share pieces of that knowledge with us. So when we are told the future in our dreams, perhaps that is our spirit guide (or even ourselves) trying to prepare us for the journey ahead.

In one of my favorite quotes from *The Time Machine*, H.G. Wells writes, "We all have our time machines, don't we? Those that take us back are memories... And those that carry us forward, are dreams." He was more right than he could have known as our dreams can literally be scenes from the future from our own timelines.

Before Einstein's theory of relativity, Wells introduced many readers to the idea of time as a measurable thing that we move along. Just as we can be described according to our position along an x-y-z matrix, denoting our width, length and depth, we also exist on a fourth plane. He said of time, "Our consciousness moves intermittently in one direction along the latter from the beginning to the end of our lives." While we control where we are along the first three planes, only spiritual beings can influence when we are. Time is set in motion the second our consciousness enters our bodies and ends when it leaves us.[11]

There are old legends in Buddhism that suggest that some of the most enlightened monks can see this fourth plane and can predict the very moment of their deaths. I first came to know about this idea in my early twenties after watching a beautiful film called *Spring, Summer, Fall, Winter...Spring*. In it, there is a scene in which an elderly Korean monk wraps himself in a cloth and lights himself on fire. He is completely alone, living in a temple on an island on a small lake. The first time I saw the scene, I thought he was committing suicide; however, the more I thought about it, the more I realized that wasn't at all what was happening. He was actually preparing his body for cremation because he knew the exact second he would die. Just before the fire actually burns him, his soul leaves.[12] I suppose it's reasonable to suggest that we choose the time of our death if we live to old age, but it becomes more difficult to accept when a person dies at a very young age. Let me share a personal story involving this.

Just a few weeks after starting sixth grade, two of my classmates named Paige and Katie were struck by a car as they held each other's hands crossing a street. One died instantly, and the other that evening at the hospital. Now, their deaths seem senseless. Eleven years is such a short time here. They had their whole lives ahead of them and countless lives to impact.

Being pretty new to the school, I barely knew the girls. Plus, I was so shy then. I had just moved to the city from a small town in the Sierra Foothills of California, where let's just say, schools did things differently, e.g., singing John Denver folk songs was part of the curriculum. I was delayed in reading and math, resulting in being forced to take remedial classes. I was so self-conscious because I felt like everyone was smarter than me.

One day, we were taking an exam. All of the desks in the class were grouped into fours. Katie was facing my direction, sitting diagonally across from me, but close enough so that our two desks touched. She tapped my foot and gestured that she wanted to look at my answers. I was scared. I didn't know what to do, so I ignored her and continued taking the test. In that moment, I was given a boost of self-esteem that I desperately needed. A bright girl like her trying to get my answers? It seemed absurd, but as a result, both my grades and confidence soon improved.

It was not long after their deaths that the class took a camping trip. On the first day, we all sat together in a large cabin and one of the camp counselors started to play the song "Circle of Life" from *The Lion King* soundtrack. As soon as the song began, I immediately thought of those girls, with the connection being that when they were still alive, our class had performed a live-action stage play based on the then recently released film. Suddenly, as I thought about them, I noticed something happening. Every kid in that room was overcome with emotion. Many were in tears. At that very moment, we were all thinking about them, every single person (well, except for the counselor, who probably thought the whole class had gone completely insane). Perhaps those girls were with us that room. Even to this day, all these decades later, I still think about them every now and then.

Now, I don't know if their accident was planned or not. If it was part of a larger plan, then the reason and consequences are a mystery. All I know is that I was practically a stranger to them, and they had an impact on me. Imagine the impact they had on those closest to them.

All of us have gifts and a purpose. The fact that you are here right now, living on Earth, is all by design. The course of seemingly random events that led human evolution to this point was maybe not so random. Even our planet's location relative to other celestial bodies may be purposeful. There are just too many coincidences to be purely chance. I'll give you just one example—solar eclipses. Our sun and moon appear exactly the same size in the sky from our perspective. Is that just a randomly cool fact? Other worlds must also have solar eclipses, right? Sure, they might have moons large enough to cover the sun; however, our solar eclipse is a perfect fit and lasts for enough time for us to appreciate it. It's so perfect, that the only light visible is the outermost region of the sun's atmosphere, called the corona. It represents the only time we can actually see this halo of white-light with our own eyes.

When the moon was first formed, it was about sixteen times closer than it is now. It has been slowly drifting away ever since, and at some point in the future, it will be too far to cover the sun. Yet today, the sun, while 400 times larger than the moon, just happens to be exactly 400 times further away from our planet. The result is one of the most spectacular natural sights we'll ever see, and it will likely only happen once in our lifetime from any one place on Earth.

Coming back to future visions, all the evidence seems to indicate that these events are shared with us in different ways, but they are not something we can control. Some method of spiritual delivery is required. So what about people who claim to be fortune-tellers or mediums, communicating with spirits and seeing the future whenever they want to? Sure, it could be possible and I am open to that, but I have yet to see any evidence to support it. Even if someone were truly psychic and connected to the spiritual realm, why would they risk interfering with your spiritual growth by spoiling your destiny? Plus, they certainly wouldn't charge money to do it. Anyone that tuned to the universe would freely give that information away if they thought you needed to hear it.

The reality is that the lucky few who did catch a glimpse of their future were granted this access temporarily, and it was orchestrated by outside forces. The universe deemed it necessary for them to see where they'd be going, just as it can show them where they've been.

CHAPTER NINE

Past Lives

There's a scene from one of my favorite reincarnation movies, *Chances Are*, where a young man named Alex fights with an older man named Philip over their love for the same woman. Alex is trying to convince Philip that he is actually the reincarnation of Louis, Philip's former best friend who died in a car accident decades earlier. Philip jokes that if that's the case, then he must be Cleopatra. However, earlier in the film, while in a new age bookstore, Alex already met a woman who claimed that she was the famous Egyptian princess.[1]

It's one of those funny examples of our ego-centric personalities at work. Deep down, we all wish that we were Cleopatra or Marc Antony or Caesar or other famous people from history. The irony is, if reincarnation really exists, then chances are that the people whose lives we inhabited lived very ordinary lives.

It reminds me of an exercise one of my psychology professors demonstrated back in university. He asked everyone to look around at our fellow classmates. Then he asked for those of us with above-average intelligence compared to the rest of the class to raise our hands. About 80 percent of the class did so. Then, he asked that everyone who felt like they would only marry once and stay married to raise our hands. Again, about 80 percent of the class responded. Well, he then made the obvious point that only 49 percent of us could technically be above average compared to our peers and that two out of three marriages ended in divorce. While it did make us look pretty foolish, it was definitely an effective exercise in humility.

Reincarnation is such a huge topic that it could easily be written about as a book all by itself, and it has been many, many times. Here, we are exploring reincarnation because it may relate closely to the NDE phenomenon.

On a personal note, the thought of reincarnation has always fascinated me. As a little kid, I would make believe I used to be a soldier in World War II. As a young adult, I even wrote an unpublished fiction book about eleventh-century crusaders who sought a fountain of youth, but rather than stop the aging process, it simply enabled them to retain their memories from life to life throughout the ages. I even remember first interpreting the song "Faithfully" by Journey as a song about souls finding each other across multiple lives. As an adult, I learned to relate to this song by its real meaning of drifting apart from your spouse while on the road, then rekindling that spark later when reunited.

I say these things as an admission that reincarnation for me was always a wonderful thought, but I only saw it as a cool theme for romantic fiction. So the idea that reincarnation is actually real was a stretch, but then on top of that, believing some of us could be made to actually recall our past lives was just too illogical. Think about it. If we were made to forget our past lives by design, then why should there be loopholes that allow us to see them? As if God could have made such an oversight.

In Greek mythology, one of the rivers of Hades is known as Lethe. Drinking from it ensured that you would forget your past life before being born again. Every soul is required to drink from these waters of forgetfulness before returning to Earth, but maybe some slipped past the guards? Is that how some retain past life memories? In all fairness, I could say it is also illogical for us to see the afterlife in NDEs, so maybe there is a method to the madness.

As it turns out, there are three main ways in which past lives are reported. There is regression hypnotherapy, the life review during an NDE, or as a memory in a young child. We will be exploring all of these types.

During my research, one name that was well-connected to this field was Dr. Ian Stevenson. He started his research back in 1967 when he headed the Division of Perceptual Studies while Chair of the Department of Psychiatry for the University of Virginia. His studies in reincarnation were focused on the memories shared by small children. Dr. Stevenson observed that the bulk of these cases were found in countries where reincarnation is embraced and talked about openly. These were places like India, Sri Lanka, and Thailand. While Dr. Stevenson was on one of his many trips to India, he discovered dozens of cases of past life memories.

One of these cases was that of a little girl named Kumkum Verma, who came from a wealthy family in a village in India. Around two years old, she started telling her parents about another life that she lived with striking detail. She claimed that she was a grandmother who lived in the city of Darbhanga (about twenty-five miles from her current village).

Within that city, she lived in a district of artisans and craftsmen. She described her son as working with a hammer and recalled her grandson's name. She even knew the name of the town her father lived in.

She then described her own home with great precision, such as an iron safe she had there, the sword that hung on the wall next to the cot she slept in, and a pet snake that she fed milk to.

While resistant at first, her father eventually investigated the matter. He had an employee who happened to live in Darbhanga and asked him to check if there were any families that matched the description. Sure enough, he was able to track them down. Every single detail was confirmed. The father traveled to meet this family only once, but he kept his daughter at home. He had great pride in his family's status and was hesitant to accept that she was once simply a blacksmith's wife. Details like that solidify this extraordinary story even more.

When Dr. Stevenson retired in 2002, one of his younger colleagues, Dr. Jim Tucker, continued his research. Dr. Tucker was a logical choice, as he also had been studying this phenomenon for decades. He is a pediatrician who specializes in cases of child reincarnation memories. In his book, *Life Before Life,* he summarizes 2,500 reincarnation cases compiled from years of research. Among them were cases investigated by his mentor, such as the one you just read. Even though 2,500 may seem like a large number, when you compare that to the one in twenty-five people who have had an NDE in the US alone, and you can start to see just how rare these cases actually are.

Interestingly, in that example from India, the time between the death of the grandmother and the birth of the daughter was just a couple of years. In fact, Dr. Tucker has found that the average interval of time for all cases is just four and a half years! He has also found that about 70 percent of the cases involve a person who died by unnatural means, such as an accident or by murder. Also, the children tended to be very bright. One study he referenced found fourteen out of fifteen with an IQ of over 100. (That one outlier got a ninety-nine, by the way).

Reading these facts, you start to wonder if reincarnation exists because the person died before they could finish their assignment here, so God brought them back. Because this isn't their first rodeo, they have a kind of muscle memory of life on Earth. You may have known some precocious kids in your class like that in grade school. Maybe you were one of them. They retain facts easier, they master music and art almost instantly, and they just sort of have a great *savoir-faire* for all of life's situations.

More recently, Dr. Tucker has focused his scope on the US in order to dismiss the notion that reincarnation cases are only found in the East and also in the hopes that more people will discover these stories if they are closer to home. Let me share two such cases that Dr. Tucker often references when lecturing about child reincarnation stories.

One case focuses on a boy named Ryan. When he was four, Ryan started telling his parents that he wanted to go back to Hollywood (his family lived in Oklahoma). After constant requests for this, the parents finally got some books on Hollywood as a way to satisfy his curiosity. Then, while looking at some old Hollywood movie stills and pictures, he said, "There's my friend, George," while pointing to a picture of the late actor George Raft. Then he added, "And that's me!" pointing to someone else beside him. The name was not listed, so they contacted Dr. Tucker to see if he could help. He contacted a Hollywood archivist to investigate. All the while, the boy continued to make very specific statements about his past life—how he lived in New York, worked on Broadway, moved to Hollywood, and started a talent agency. He even recalled that the street he lived on had "rock" in the name. Well, the archivist eventually came back with information from the Academy of Motion Picture Arts and Sciences. The man in the picture was Marty Martin, a relatively unknown person in Hollywood, yet all of the details matched up. Incidentally, the street with "rock" in its name was "Rochurst". In total, over fifty statements were confirmed.[2]

In another well-known story, there was a boy named James Leininger. At just two, he started to talk about being a World War II fighter pilot. He would constantly draw pictures of planes on fire crashing into the ground. Strangely, he would also sign them "James 3." He was so passionate about this that his father took him to an air museum, and naturally, the young boy was completely focused on the World War II-era planes.

James explained that while he was stationed on a ship, he was a pilot of a Corsair that had crashed after being shot in the engine. His father asked what the name of the boat was, to which James replied, "Natoma." Thinking that was a strange name for a boat operated by the US military, the father said, "That sounds like a Japanese boat." James insisted it was American. While looking through a book on Iwo Jima, James indicated the location where his plane had crashed. His father asked who was there, and James replied, "Me, James." His father asked, "Who was with you?" His son responded, "Jack Larson."

Well, as it turned out, there was a person named Jack Larson stationed on the USS *Natoma Bay* at Iwo Jima, and there was just one man from that crew who died there after his engine was shot. It also turned out Jack Larson was remarkably still alive, albeit very old, so James' father went to meet him. Jack said he was in the plane just next to the one that was shot down. The pilot's name was James Huston, Jr. It finally made sense why James Leininger kept signing his drawings "James 3." He was, in fact, the third James, spiritually speaking.[3]

Dr. Tucker has also found that the cause of death from a previous life can influence the phobias we have in our current one. He even found that people who were the opposite sex in their previous life sometimes still identified with their previous gender. I wonder if these types of observations could help to explain why some identical twins, who share 100 percent of the same DNA and grow up in the same house, have different preferences, such as for food, even as infants. Their taste buds should be identical, so their sensitivity to different flavors should also be.[4]

These observations feed into the longstanding debate in psychology about nature versus nurture. The philosopher John Locke popularized the idea that we come into this world with a *Tabula Rasa*, a Latin expression meaning "clean slate." It suggests that all of our thoughts, likes, and motivations develop through life experiences after we are born. Some psychologists supported elements of this theory, such as Sigmund Freud, who believed our personalities, behaviors, and complexes were developed by childhood experiences and trauma.

Others, such as Carl Jung, believed they were rooted somewhere else, somewhere much deeper. Jung called this source the collective unconscious. While the individual's unconscious mind is the result of personal experiences that are stored subconsciously, the collective unconscious refers to the ancestral memory that we inherit. These hidden forces help to shape our behaviors by influencing how we react to various situations. Jung saw distinct, recognizable patterns that we each exhibit that help identify our inner selves. He called these patterns *archetypes*, a concept many consider to be one of the greatest contributions to modern psychology.

Jung believed strongly that discovering which archetypes were part of you was imperative in your journey to self-actualization. He believed that they helped you to better understand who you truly are and your unique role in the universe. It was through the process of *individuation* that brought the unconscious parts of your identity into consciousness. When that integration was complete, it meant that your best, highest, and most unique version of yourself could be fully realized. This totality of the self is known as your *psyche*, a word of Greek origin that literally translates to "soul."

Let's now briefly explore reincarnation as seen through regression hypnotherapy. One rather famous psychiatrist named Dr. Brian Weiss has written books on this subject. For him, there was a single moment that made him a believer in the afterlife. It started when he was working with a patient, trying to pinpoint the cause of one of her phobias. During one of his therapy sessions, Dr. Weiss was attempting to trace the source by having the patient recall moments from her earliest memories. Suddenly, she was describing seeing herself as an eighteen-year-old girl named Aronda with blond, braided hair. She described living in a desert valley with mountains in the background that supplied the water to a nearby well. She observed ancient buildings with columns and primitive carrying baskets. She said this took place thousands of years ago.

At first, he dismissed this. It was probably part of her subconscious memory of a movie. However, she then made reference to Dr. Tucker's deceased mother and son. She described them and even the condition that his infant son had with his heart that led to his early death. He was shocked! This was information he hadn't even shared with his extended family. A skeptic might say she looked this information up online, but being as it was in the 1980s, it predated the internet.[5]

In the years since, he has helped many more patients overcome their fears and anxiety by locating the original source of their issue. He has made appearances on television, like on *The Oprah Show*. In one of those episodes, he and some of his patients revealed some remarkable discoveries.

One of them was with a patient he worked with named Jodi. She had an irrational and intense fear of dolls. To most of us, that would seem kind of comical, but to her, it was very serious. After exhausting the possibility of the origin of her fear happening in her current life, Dr. Weiss helped her to see her past life. During her hypnosis, she was accompanied by her spirit guide, a male spirit who happened to be her deceased grandfather. She saw herself in a car that had just been in a wreck. She had died in that accident, leaving her two babies in the backseat of the car crying for her. She floated above this scene, and while she knew everything was going to be okay, her babies were too young to process that and just wanted their mother back. She was made to see that they would grow up to be just fine.

Next, Dr. Weiss helped Jodi connect to an experience she had in her current life. When she was eighteen months old, she had to be taken to a hospital, and her parents had to wait outside. The nurse gave her a doll to comfort her. In that room, she was scared and heard the cries of the babies who were in nearby rooms. Her subconscious connected those cries to the cries of her own babies from her past life that she left behind. The association of the doll she was clutching onto during that moment led to her current fear. Her newfound understanding helped her to overcome this.[6]

The origin of phobias can be formed from complex

associations like this, but more often, the source is much simpler. The current research suggests there is often a link between the fear of the environment that led to one's death in a previous life. It could be a fatal drowning, a fire, an animal attack, a plane crash, or other specific things. Let me be clear, though. The majority of the time, phobias originate from a person's current life, usually from a childhood experience. So we shouldn't jump to conclusions that all fears originate from past lives. It is much more likely something recent that made you that way.

The final type of past life recollection happens during the NDE. As the soul is watching their current life review, they sometimes will also get to see scenes from their past lives, too. It could be argued that because of that, these cases are a bit more convincing because we know that life reviews seen by near-death survivors are authentic, so it stands to reason that past life reviews should also be just as real. I'd like to share two cases of this type of experience.

First, there is the case of Vi Horton. During a lengthy cardiac arrest in 1971, she had an NDE with many of the classic elements present, such as the life review and the tunnel. As she came through the end of the tunnel, she described stepping into a "beautiful valley with a river flowing and a green pasture." There she was greeted by many different souls, including her mother and grandparents and even a brother that she never knew existed but was later confirmed by her still-living father.

When she came to the part of her NDE relating to her life review, she described it being a panorama of her life. Just as in earlier examples, she was both watching and reliving these scenes. However, in her case, she saw what she described as "filaments of light" that connected scenes of her current life with moments from past ones. One of these moments involved an event that happened when she was three years old. She had run out into the street where a car was forced to brake to avoid hitting her. There happened to be another three-year-old child in that car who was thrown against the dashboard and killed. (This took place before seat belts were commonplace). Now, the filament for this event connected to a scene from a previous life where Vi was riding in the front seat of a horse-drawn carriage. A young child ran out in front of it, forcing the driver to come to an abrupt stop that resulted in Vi being thrown over and killed. The child who ran in front of that carriage was the reincarnated child who was thrown against the car dashboard in Vi's current life.[7]

For reasons beyond our understanding, these two souls needed to both experience the same guilt of causing the other's death, almost like a cosmic balancing act.

Next, let's revisit the case of Dr. Rajiv Parti, focusing on the reincarnation portion of his extraordinary experience. He saw his life review while traveling through the tunnel. It was there where he was made to also see his past lives. He described two of them quite vividly. In one life, he was a nineteenth-century poppy seed farmer in Afghanistan who eventually became addicted to opioids. In another, he was a rich landowner who would whip the peasants for disobedience. Before having this NDE, he suffered from chronic pain, anger, and addiction. During this past life experience, he could clearly see where those characteristics were coming from and was able to completely change his life and become a better and healthier person. Dr. Weiss was able to help Dr. Rajiv explore more of these connections between lives through regression hypnotherapy sessions.[8]

The idea of reincarnation is exciting and comforting. You might be thinking, somewhat jokingly, "Yes, I get another shot at this!" The spiritual side sees it as an opportunity to continue its learning.

You might also be wondering if your loved ones move on before you die or if you will have the chance to see them again. We have already established through the extensive research of Dr. Tucker and Dr. Stevenson that the average time between lives is just four and a half years. Of course, we sometimes live much longer than that after our loved ones pass, so does that mean they have already moved on to other lives by the time we die? Is that why sometimes older couples die within months of each other? They want to move on together? Perhaps, but maybe we are putting too much emphasis on time being a factor.

Assuming time exists only in the physical realm. When we travel from heaven to inhabit our lives here, we pick a point in time to jump into, live out that timeline, and then return. To the spiritual beings, wouldn't we appear to instantly return? While we can only speculate as to the rules and limitations of this spiritual dimension, two things are clear: we know this place exists and we know it's responsible for us.

Even the most renowned names in the scientific community concede that some force, unknown to them, is responsible for time and space. Sure, we can trace our expanding universe back to a singular event called the Big Bang. We can even describe what the conditions looked like moments after the event occurred in great detail, but what about the exact moment it happened or, better yet, the moments before it happened. (Someone out there is whispering, "It's when God divided by zero.")

Even if the Big Bang is the source of where time began, some form of energy was around before that. Remember that energy cannot be created or destroyed, it can only be transformed. There are some who believe that our reality is just a small part of a larger landscape of existence. The prevailing theory that may help support that idea is called string theory. Proponents of it believe that the fundamental constituents that make up all things in the universe is something that we can't see because they are smaller than the tiniest particles that we can measure.

Before diving any deeper into this subject, it's time for a quick crash course in chemistry. All physical matter is built from atoms. Forming the center of an atom are subatomic particles called protons and neutrons. Moving around that center are tiny electrons, traveling around 1 percent the speed of light. (That may sound slow, but it's fast enough to circumnavigate the globe in 18.4 seconds!) The number of those protons and neutrons can be added together to determine the atomic weight of all known elements. For example, oxygen has eight of each, producing an atomic weight of 15.999. Inside of those subatomic particles are quarks, representing the extent to which our technology allows us to see.

Coming back to string theory, it is the belief that inside of those quarks are tiny, dancing filaments of vibrating energy. The different vibrations produced by these energy strings create the subatomic particles of every atom. Just as the strings of a guitar make music, these strings create a cosmic orchestra, responsible for everything that we know (and don't know).

However, the mathematics of string theory don't add up in a three-dimensional universe. They only work in a universe with ten dimensions of space and one dimension of time. Therefore, the Big Bang was only responsible for the expansion of the physical universe that we see and move around in. Thus, our perception is limited to three-dimensional objects because that is our purview.

Carl Sagan explained this concept brilliantly by borrowing elements from a nineteenth-century book called

Flatland: A Romance of Many Dimensions. The idea is that we are able to see our three-dimensional world as well as the two-dimensional world of Flatland. Those flat people could not see us, but they could see the result of any changes we made to their world. If we picked one of them up, to the other residents of Flatland, it would seem as though their friend had just vanished into thin air. That's because they can only see in two-dimensional space. To us, we simply brought their two-dimensional friend into our three-dimensional world. This concept can be expanded to help describe how we would react to being taken into fourth or fifth-dimensional space by beings that reside there.[9]

If this premise is true, it would mean that all our loved ones could be there waiting on the other side, regardless of time. The only reason they would not be there is if they are in a different realm or dimension because we must first fulfill the prerequisite learning to access their level.

This and other theories help explain timelessness, but there are some observations that contradict this premise. For instance, one of Dr. Moody's children told him that God said that when we die, we must stay there and wait for our loved ones before moving on.[10] To wait for something implies time is present. There have also been accounts of fellow spiritual beings being overjoyed at the person's return and inquiring about their experience on Earth, suggesting we were gone for some time. There's also the simple fact that we appear to only see deceased loved ones there and not the ones that are still alive. This sort of conflicts with the idea of linear timelines being exclusive to our reality. So perhaps there are rules even in heaven that we don't fully understand. That's okay. I can wait to find out. Somehow, I think everything will be fine and work out exactly as planned.

CHAPTER TEN

Gifts from the Other Side

Everyone who has come back from an NDE brings with them a special gift. For most, this gift could simply be the knowledge they now have of what lies ahead for all of us and a new set of priorities to follow in their life. Also, they no longer have a fear of death, and in fact, they look forward to that moment when they can return to their spiritual home.

When at a funeral, we are taught to say things like, "They are in a better place now" or "They have finally found peace." These statements are kind of mocked nowadays because they seem inauthentic and cliché. The irony is that they are about the truest words one can say in that moment. Our loved ones who pass on are in a state of blissful existence that is so far beyond ours that it is hard for us to relate or understand it. We may feel guilt, anger, sadness, or other human emotions. They feel nothing but unconditional love for us and remain connected to us spiritually.

Knowing this divine love awaits all of us should hopefully bring some solace. Since this indescribable joy can only be felt in heaven, it's no wonder NDE-ers often wish to remain there, even if it means leaving their families behind. Their human side feels guilty about this, but the beauty of their true home is just too much for them to walk away from.

Some are so completely changed from the experience that their life goals suddenly conflict with their spouses, and they end up having to separate as a result. There are many stories of successful businessmen and women who had an NDE, then suddenly gave most of their money away, leaving their still money-driven spouses confused and angry. For others, the event rekindles and even strengthens their relationships as they bond in a new shared vision of their life goals and what makes them truly happy.

Even when someone is close to death but doesn't have an NDE, we still see this change in them. People who have been through life-saving surgeries and organ transplants often wake up appreciating life more and tend to show more love and gratitude. We attribute that to the reality of getting another chance at life. Perhaps that is it. Or maybe their subconscious is remembering the effects of an NDE they weren't aware even happened, kind of like how we only remember our dreams some of the time, but even when we forget them, the emotions we felt in our dreams tend to linger.

We build human constructs of what should make us happy. Things that we think other people expect us to have to determine if we are successful in life. We must acquire lots of wealth, conform to recognized standards of beauty, and settle for groupthink just to fit in. It's easy to see why so many people get depressed when they discover that they are unique, a trait that should be celebrated. Happiness is much easier to achieve than checking boxes on that superficial list.

Coming back with a clear pathway to real happiness could be seen as a gift in itself, but for a precious few, there are other gifts they return with—enhanced abilities.

One of the more common and measurable after-effects of an NDE is an increase in intelligence. Some recall getting their IQ prior to the NDE and then seeing their score jump over twenty points upon return.

In one case, a former mechanic named Tom was crushed underneath a car for about fifteen minutes, cutting off his air supply for that duration. He had a high school level education and joked that the diploma was only given to him because he was nineteen, and they wanted him to leave. After the accident, it took him about three days to recover to the point where he could communicate with the hospital staff, and almost immediately, he showed signs of increased intelligence. He started talking about quantum physics, wave functions, and other advanced topics. He was referencing equations and quotes of people and things that he didn't previously know anything about. One quote he had written was, "A new scientific truth does not triumph by convincing its opponents and making them see the light, but rather because its opponents eventually die, and a new generation grows up that is familiar with it." Was the scientific truth in question about sharing proof of the afterlife? He wondered where this idea came from. It turns out that it was said by theoretical physicist and Nobel Prize winner Max Planck.[1] It seemed as though Tom was now the fortunate recipient of advanced knowledge courtesy of the universe.

Then there are reports of telepathic capabilities that some have returned with. In a rather amusing story, Robert Bare revealed that he could now sometimes hear others' thoughts and recalled a recent event where he was standing in line at Walmart and suddenly heard the phrase "Chinese Dragon Red" in his head. He looked at the woman standing next to him and instantly realized that she had painted a wall in her house this color. He asked the woman, "Did you just paint a wall Chinese Dragon Red?" She responded with shock, "Yes, I did! How did you know?" He suddenly realized it was probably a mistake to reveal that to her. When he left the store to go to his car, the woman and some others followed him outside, probably thinking he was some kind of stalker or something.[2]

There are other fantastic stories of people coming back with newly heightened senses. Some can still occasionally smell the heavenly scent from their NDEs.[3] The sense of sight can also be enhanced with cases of being able to see the energy associated with individuals in the form of auras.[4]

There is another type of gift that is far more common than the ones just mentioned. That is the miraculous healing that patients experience after an NDE.

Dr. Penny Satori has written about some of these unexplained healing events. One of these cases happened during her residency with a patient who had Cerebral Palsy. This condition kept his hand in a permanent cup-like formation where his fingers were pointing toward his wrist. This man was sixty years old at the time and was born with this condition. Yet after having an NDE, his hand could freely open and stretch. The physicians explained to Dr. Satori that being in that position for so long, his tendons should have been in a permanently contracted position, and only an operation to release those tendons would even make it possible for the hand to stretch out again. Even the man's sister confirmed this was the first time in her life that she ever saw him use that hand.[5]

In another case, renowned cardiac surgeon Dr. Lloyd Rudy described a man who came in on anticoagulation drugs because his blood had been clotting. To help him, they needed to stop the bleeding, and they tried every method available to do so. They had just about given up when the entire staff in the room felt a presence enter. For a moment, everybody just froze, wondering what was going on. Immediately, the bleeding stopped and the patient made an instant recovery. This, along with many other unexplainable situations, convinced Dr. Rudy of a higher power.[6]

We hear about medical marvels all the time. The family of the patient usually calls it a miracle, and if the family is religious, then they will sometimes say that it was their prayers that produced that miracle. I have always credited these cases as simply evidence of the strong willpower of the patient's desire to live along with the skill of the doctors.

However, many NDE-ers claim that while they were on the other side, they could actually see these prayers visualized. Some are able to see the Earth with beams of light shooting out from it. Other times, they can see crystal orbs above the people making the prayers.[7] They are able to feel the prayers that were specifically directed toward them. This usually occurs while God or other light beings are trying to persuade them to return to Earth.

One might wonder why it is that only some people come back with enhanced abilities. We know that in our spiritual form, we have enhanced senses, such as telepathy and universal knowledge. As human beings, we are limited to only our five senses, but the soul has many more, and perhaps these lucky survivors retained part of these extrasensory perceptions. Maybe as we become more in tune with our souls, we can develop them too.

For the rest of us, we also get a gift and we didn't even have to die to receive it. That would be our access to hearing these awesome experiences about the afterlife.

Those who do eventually decide to share their personal accounts touch the lives of untold millions of people. This is particularly true in the modern age, where all one has to do is post their experience online, and people across the globe can see it. Their ripple touches us, and in doing so, allows us to start our own ripples that touch others.

In this day and age, the majority of our interactions are online over phones and computers. Many employees work remotely from home offices. Personal relationships have become largely dependent on technology. It can be a bit concerning because physical interactions seem so important for our spiritual growth. That being said, we can still do good things virtually. In fact, technology has made doing this easier by helping to shine light on causes that would otherwise go unnoticed. For example, when Russia attacked Ukraine in early 2022, just look at how quickly the world united in their support of the Ukrainian people, through financial support and helping its refugees find safe havens. It was a different story when we look back just a few decades prior to social media, before we could share images and videos from our phones.

My wife was also a refugee. Only she was from Laos, fleeing the small, Southeast Asian county as just a baby in her mother's arms in 1985. This was part of the aftermath of the US withdrawal from Vietnam in the 1970s, as the civil war against American-supported governments in Laos fell to communist Pathet Lao with the help of the Vietnamese military. The newly installed government would send armed personnel to my wife's family home to demand money and assets in exchange for survival, claiming the money was paying for their own safety. This was the case for many families. The government was killing its own people. (During this period, about one-tenth of the 3 million Laotian citizens left their homes behind in hopes of a better life.)

Her family escaped by crossing the Mekong River into Thailand amidst the gunfire and chaos, then finding a refugee camp with the help of the United Nations. Due to the high rates of disease in the camps there, they were moved to the Philippines before ultimately finding a new home in the US.

Now chances are you never heard of these events. There were no smartphones around back then or even access to the internet. We would never stand for these atrocities if they were happening today. For reasons like this, I do see modern communication methods as a great thing in the fight for human rights.

The internet is also responsible for introducing me and so many others to NDEs. I wish every person could take ten to twenty minutes out of their day to watch someone share their story with an open mind. Wonderful things will happen.

We think of our soul as just a small part of us. Something that fits inside the crevices of the brain or maybe hugging onto the heart. The reality is that your soul is the largest part of you, and it is your human self that is just a small part of it. So small, in fact, that our lives are just a fleeting moment in the timeline of our soul's existence. When we die, our soul has no trouble leaving behind our bag of bones. Deep inside, the only things we truly care about are the lessons that helped shape our soul's character and the love we gave and received. Those are the things we carry with us. Here on Earth, we forget that this is all an illusion designed for our souls to grow. We can lose track of our priorities in all the cloudy minutiae of our chaotic lives. Well, it doesn't have to be so complex. Remember how honeybees have that solar compass that always shows them the direction of the sun? Well, we have something even better; a moral compass that always shines in the direction of love. It is when we follow that path through simple, kind gestures that we are most truly aligned to our soul.

CHAPTER ELEVEN

Where Science Meets Fiction

Many people think of Earth as their permanent home and the only place where life exists. Yet there is still so much we don't know about the universe that it is arrogant to believe our planet is alone in this category. Considering that we've only explored and charted about 5 percent of our own oceans, who are we to make such bold affirmations? Just look at our solar system and how much we've only recently discovered. It wasn't until 2005 that we finally penetrated the thick gold atmosphere of Titan to discover another world with liquid lakes on its surface. Only in 2015 did we finally do a flyby of Pluto to reveal what many thought would be a cold, dead world was actually very much alive with mountains, cryovolcanoes, a nitrogen-rich atmosphere, and even blue skies. We still debate as to whether life exists or has ever existed on Mars, which is literally one of our neighbors. All of that in a small sample of worlds orbiting a single star, of which there are over one hundred billion more sitting in the Milky Way alone. When you consider the immensity of that and the endless possibilities that come with it, you start to feel very small indeed. Carl Sagan famously said that there are more stars in the heavens than grains of sands on all of Earth's beaches.

There is a term in astronomy called the habitable zone, aka the Goldilocks zone, that claims if a planet is positioned at just the right proximity to its parent star, then it is more likely to have liquid water on its surface and therefore has a greater chance of supporting life. We think this because those are the conditions needed for us to survive. The irony here is that, besides Earth, all of the places in our solar system that have the best chance for life are far beyond this habitable zone, many being moons of Jupiter and Saturn. It just demonstrates how little we know about the conditions needed for life to exist, in physical form or otherwise.

Because there are so many possible scenarios out there, science fiction writers have explored lots of them. Some of their stories gravitate more toward absurdity than others, but the well-thought-out ones can appear reasonable because they are grounded in real scientific theories. So when ideas like wormholes, fourth-dimensional beings and string theory are used to help explain NDEs, it can be easy to dismiss them because they are also invoked in stories of fantasy so often. Hopefully, the line between these is clear.

With all that being said, there is a remarkable realization that I thought about the more I researched NDEs. It will probably sound a bit crazy at first, but hear me out on this. If our souls are light beings from another world, then that technically makes us all aliens. Our bodies are biologically from Earth, yet our consciousness is not from Earth. It only inhabits human form to interact in our physical environment. Perhaps our souls can inhabit other alien bodies on other distant worlds too.

So that's it, somebody call NASA! Our search for extraterrestrials is over! Probably not exactly what they had in mind, but then again, what were we expecting? It's funny because Hollywood got away with portraying aliens as very human-like for so long. Just take a human and add some green paint, or some fur, or pointed ears, and presto, an alien! There is a psychology term to describe this called *anthropomorphism*. It is the tendency for us to apply human traits to things that aren't human. It's probably a subconscious trait rather than deliberate, so I'll give us a pass on this one.

More recently, movies have been better about this. One of my favorite depictions of an alien is one that John Carpenter created for us. No, I'm not talking about *The Thing,* that film still freaks me out. I'm actually talking about *Starman,* where the alien appears as a ball of pure light energy, which creates a human host from the DNA of another human and transfers his consciousness into him.[1]

That may have been a science fiction fantasy, but some of the most brilliant scientific minds are talking right now about theoretical ways of transferring our consciousness into other hosts. One idea is to place our consciousness into devices the size of thumb drives and thrust them into space faster than a human body could ever travel in an effort to advance space exploration capabilities. Another idea is to create android-like bodies in which our consciousness would be placed, thus expanding the lifespan of a human exponentially.[2]

Now before we go down this road, haven't we seen this played out before on old episodes of *Star Trek*? Did it ever end well? (To find out, watch the 1966 episode *What Are Little Girls Made Of?* Spoiler: the android goes crazy, and most of the humans die in agony).[3]

With techniques like neuroimaging, we are closer than ever to mapping all of the brain to its relevant functions. Once that mapping is complete and we can recreate the human brain in a laboratory, the next logical step is to transfer ourselves into these artificial brains, but if the soul leaves the moment the body dies, what exactly is it that we are preserving? It is certainly not our consciousness. Our soul is only here for a temporary assignment and probably can't wait to return home. What transfers into the host would merely be a facsimile of the physical brain, not the mind. That little subtlety makes all the difference in the end.

This whole debate seems like something that would be discussed by celebrity physicists like Brian Greene or Neil Degrasse Tyson. Incidentally, I'm an avid listener of *StarTalk*, hosted by Tyson and Chuck Nice. They explore the astrophysics and theoretical concepts that make up our universe in relatable ways and with humor.[4] At a time filled with so much anger, division, and politics, it is a nice escape for many who just want to learn more about science and maybe laugh a little along the way.

I should probably mention that Tyson has publically shrugged off the notion of NDEs. I imagine his mentor, Carl Sagan, probably felt the same. Growing up in the 1980s and '90s, *Cosmos* was mandatory viewing, courtesy of my mother. Sagan was an extraordinary man with an extraordinary mind who taught us to look up to the stars and realize just how many amazing possibilities exist out there, as seen from this pale blue dot we live on. Even so, Sagan dismissed the existence of a higher power, believing that we human beings control our own destiny and that when we die, that is the end of our journey. He even promoted the now-debunked theory that the light and tunnel phases of an NDE were derived from our early memories of passing through the birth canal.[5] That is okay. Even though he was wrong in this area, I still love and respect him. We have to remember that it is okay to appreciate and admire those with differing opinions. Sagan romanticized astronomy and helped cultivate generations of dreamers and science lovers.

In the moments immediately after his death, all of the answers to the universe that he spent his career searching for would have been revealed to him in an instant. A spectacular moment indeed! Along with this cosmic knowledge would be the realization of the positive impact he had on so many lives. And yet, there would be something else that would consume his curious mind over all of the scientific discoveries bestowed upon him—that love was the binding force that connects all life in the universe.

CHAPTER TWELVE

Conclusions and Practical Applications

So what are the final conclusions to be drawn from all of these stories? And how might these conclusions apply to our own lives? First of all, let's review the highlights. We are eternal light beings experiencing a temporary human existence. We come from a spiritual dimension to learn lessons about the human condition. We are only here for a short time, and then we return to our true home of love, light, and acceptance. When we die, there are three possible scenarios. First, we are told to return to our bodies as it is not yet our time. Second, we are given the choice to stay or return. Lastly, our time is up, and we transition completely into that heavenly existence. Perhaps even in that last scenario, we may choose to come back to Earth through reincarnation to inhabit more lives if there are more lessons to learn.

In the heavenly realm, we have access to a universal database of knowledge that allows us to understand every aspect of existence. We communicate with each other telepathically as soon as a thought is conceived. We can travel by floating, walking, or by thought, teleporting from one spot to the next as we desire. We are all endowed with unique gifts that we bring with us to Earth, and while we have specific goals to achieve here, the unifying message is to simply be a kind person to everyone we meet and to enjoy our time here because our lives are precious. All life is.

So were the collection of stories from this book enough evidence to convince a skeptic that there is an afterlife? That is for you to decide, but they were for the people who had those NDEs, their families, and the many doctors, nurses, and anesthesiologists who were witnesses to them. They were also enough for me as a former skeptic. It is true that my belief system has always been rooted in science and logic. That hasn't changed. I'm still and always will be a lover and student of all sciences. Part of the intention of this book was to show that these two schools of thought are not mutually exclusive. In fact, one can help explain the other in mutually beneficial ways. Einstein spent his life searching for the so-called God Equation—a formula that could link everything together.

So now that we know there is an afterlife, what do we do with this information? For me, I thought, "Well, I need to go change the world! This should be on the headlines of every news article! This is bigger than politics, sports, or even aliens!"

Others have had similar reactions. Remember that lovely woman with the inner tube story from the first chapter? She explained it best. She initially had the same instinct as I did, feeling compelled to share her news and leave an indelible mark for the world to see. When she had asked about the purpose of her life, God said, "You will help me by showing love to people." Wondering what exactly he meant by this, she thought, "Do I go around hugging everybody that I meet?" She later joked that an instruction manual would be nice.

It was many years after her NDE that she learned what that meant for her. It was just about being a kinder and more compassionate person. Fulfilling her purpose did not require her to be a big shot CEO who runs a billion dollar company or some ultra-rich celebrity with book and movie deals and a legion of Twitter followers. She said, "It's in all of the everyday interactions with people just to show kindness and love. Be a good listener. That sort of thing. It's really quite easy, and it makes you feel good too."[1]

So is being a good person all there is to life's purpose? When asked about the meaning of their lives, everyone is essentially told the same message: to show love to everyone. Of course, we each have more specific tasks to complete as well, but showing love seems to be the constant thread that binds us all. Some NDE-ers have actually shared how they were expecting more, like, "That's it? All you need is love?" The omnipotent God who knows everything that is, was, and ever will be is saying that the dogma of life can be summed up by one line from a Beatles song. It does seem overly simple, but sometimes the hardest things to do in life can be the simplest things to understand.

We overcomplicate our lives by prioritizing nonsensical things, unrelated to our spiritual growth, above what's really important. There are so many cases of the life review where the person laughs along with God at how seriously they took life all the time, when all along, it was just about love and having a good time.

While this message is crystal clear, knowing it and applying it are two different things. It takes a lot of spiritual strength and willpower to align your thoughts and behaviors to this high form of love.

The main obstacle is your great nemesis—the ego. For him, it is never enough. You can try to quench his thirst and the two of you will have fleeting moments of satisfaction, but in the end, he never cared about you or your happiness, he only cared about himself and how others perceived him.

For me, I keep him locked up most of the time, but every now and then he slips out. Therefore, I still get angry sometimes. I still have arguments with my spouse over silly things. It's just that now, I usually catch myself almost immediately and realize how foolish I'm behaving. I used to be too proud to apologize, but now it's easier. I just listen to my conscience and ask myself if I am being the best version of myself in that moment. If my spouse is the instigator, then I ask her the same question. I do it somewhat lightheartedly and not in a condescending way. Afterward, we both just smile because the answer is so obvious. I only wish I could have learned this secret formula years earlier.

Incidentally, one of the top things people argue about is money—a human construct that is of no consequence in the afterlife. Of course, we don't live in a Star Trek-like utopian future where money is a thing of the past. We actually have to work to survive, and as such, our jobs are where we spend a good chunk of our lives. Therefore, enjoying what we do is essential, but so is having perspective of everything else.

I used to get so stressed over deadlines, that I would end up working late into the evenings, ignoring something of greater importance than my work obligations. I shared a home with a healthy, beautiful family that loved me. That was where my free time and energy should be spent.

At the time, I was performing dual roles at my

company. I was managing the global training operations for one of our products while also working as a full-time senior training consultant. I was operating beyond my bandwidth, in part because I cared about our customers, but also because I was hopeful for a promotion, but at what cost? Why was I working twelve hours a day, when 100 years from now, no one will care if I completed some project on time for a company that no longer exists? After all, did I want my epitaph to say, "He was a hard worker who always hit his numbers" or "He was a loving father, husband, brother, son, and friend"? Work is important, but it must be balanced with your life. At the time, I couldn't see that. All I could see was a promotion that I felt entitled to, so I had put all my effort into that, believing that was my only path forward. Eventually, the day came when the promotion would be decided and it ended up going to someone else. I was shattered. Part of me was happy for my colleague, because they are a wonderful person, but I felt lost at the same time. I had no idea where I went from there. It was the very next day when another door opened and a new opportunity emerged. It's funny because doors are always opening, it's just we're often too blind to see them. I stepped through this one and a great career change too place as a result, allowing for a more flexible schedule.

While it is not required in your spiritual journey, having a job you enjoy that generates enough income to live comfortably will make opportunities for introspection far easier to have. It harkens back to basic psychology and Abraham Maslow's hierarchy of needs. Maslow believed a set of prerequisites about our state of mind must first be satisfied before we are ready to move from the lower areas of this pyramid to the top in our attempt at seeking self-actualization. Many famous psychologists believed this to be the fundamental motivation of all human beings. Carl Jung summed up the idea nicely when he said, "The privilege of a lifetime is to become who you truly are."

The wonderful thing is that you can change who you are and your perception of the world any time you want. We have this concept of a New Year's resolution where we make a promise to improve ourselves in the coming year. Well, why wait for next year? In fact, why even wait for tomorrow? You can change your attitude and your behavior whenever you're ready. It's difficult, trust me, I know! I have a long way to go in my own journey. Yet it feels so good when you can just snap your fingers, swallow your pride, and choose to be the better you right then and there.

We are so fortunate to be at the right place and the right time to listen to these NDEs and discover that we are stronger than we ever imagined. To realize our lives are blessed and that every decision that we've ever made has led us to where we are right now in our path toward reaching our human potential.

Part of the responsibility that comes with this higher version of you is realizing that everyone is at different stages in their journey. Some are further along than others. Some will make decisions that you don't agree with. They might say or do things that hurt you. Even so, you have to try to continue being the best version of yourself. You can't change others, but perhaps some of your goodness might just rub off on them. We've seen men and women change the course of history by doing just that. We all know it as the golden rule, that maxim that instructs us to treat others as we would want to be treated. There is an old quote attributed to Mohandas Gandhi: "Be the change you wish to see in the world." That sentence is, in fact, a paraphrasing of a more deeply worded message from his writings published in 1913:

"We but mirror the world. All the tendencies present in the outer world are to be found in the world of our body. If we could change ourselves, the tendencies in the world would also change. As a man changes his own nature, so does the attitude of the world change towards him… We need not wait to see what others do."[2]

I guess that is too long to be a meme or fit on a novelty t-shirt. Nevertheless, it summarizes well the overall message that near-death survivors relay when they return here. Remember what Erica was told: "You are the rock. You are the light. You are the ripple that affects mankind."[3]

In many ways, our society has made great strides over the last few decades in terms of how we treat one another. Our workforce is more diverse than ever before, and we've started to see more races and religions reflected in politics and in the entertainment industry. And yet, in spite of all the progress we have made in our diversity of race, we seem to have stepped backward in embracing diversity of thought. We used to celebrate different points of view, but now many people expect and demand only one view. It seems like there is so much judgment these days that you can only be friends with those who align to your beliefs 100 percent, and as a result, friendships have been lost over inconsequential things like political beliefs. Then there is the anonymity of the internet, where you can't scroll down more than a few comments on a post or video until you see the hate and division on full display. The media adds fuel to this fire by seeking to destroy reputations any chance it gets. While a lot of this is probably just fake outrage done for attention, the ripple it makes is very real. It's easy to see why so many are cynical toward humanity.

If NDEs teach us anything, it is that we all come from the same place—the same source of all life. That effectively makes us all brothers and sisters. Your best friend, your schoolteacher, your colleague at work, your classmate who is made fun of, and the homeless person at the park are people who come from the exact same place as you. They all have a purpose here and chose to be here. When you consider that, it will change your outlook on everything.

I see enough people doing good deeds that my faith in us remains strong. In my neighborhood, there is a woman who paints hearts over graffiti and picks up trash in her spare time. On the side of a busy street, somebody painted the words, "Everything is going to be okay." In the final days of writing this book, someone wrote in chalk at a local shopping center, "Be the reason someone smiles." If you look for them, the signs are all around us.

I recall in my senior year of high school, I met someone in my anthropology class who practiced Zoroastrianism. It was the first time I'd ever heard of that religion, but I still remember a simple teaching he told me that was the heart of it: "Good Thoughts. Good Words. Good Deeds." What a simple, perfect combination of words to live by.

During my decade as a training consultant, I traveled to a lot of amazing places and met many interesting people. The one constant I noticed in every place I went was the kindness I received as a stranger. It didn't matter if it was the heart of India or the most affluent neighborhoods in Europe. When we show kindness to others, more often than not, that kindness will be reciprocated.

On several of these business trips, my family would be in tow. I recall on one of them, we stayed a night in a small city in Germany called Cochem. It is a fairytale location, complete with a medieval castle on a hill and a river flowing underneath it. I had gotten up early in the morning, several hours before sunrise, and decided to walk outside to get some fresh country air. It felt a bit strange, being that I was totally alone strolling around this city. After ten minutes or so, I started walking back when I noticed a bright object darting across the sky. It was a shooting star! Believe it or not, this was the first I'd ever seen. It was probably there for a couple of seconds, but it felt much longer, and in that moment, I thought about the serendipity of it all. Here I was in my mid-thirties with my family on another continent thousands of miles from home. The whole of Europe was asleep, and this meteor hits our atmosphere at that precise moment, illuminating in a glorious blaze seemingly just for me. It was a magical moment that gave me a taste of the cosmic peace so many have described.

When we meet God, some people say he resembles a star. If I have any control over how he'll appear to me, then I'd love to see him in that form. It makes sense that God should resemble our sun. The sun brings life and warmth, but it does more than that. It is also symbolic of hope and a bright future. Just look at all of the cultural references. Many popular songs have been written about it in this way, such as "Here Comes the Sun", "I Can See Clearly Now", and "Aquarius / Let the Sunshine In". The last example, in particular, was an anthem for an entire generation in the 1960s that conveyed a message of hope and optimism for better times ahead.

During his "I Have a Dream" speech in 1963, Martin Luther King, Jr. famously said that the Emancipation Proclamation came as a "great beacon light of hope" and "as a joyous daybreak to end the long night of their captivity." His entire speech is filled with words and symbolism like this.[4] Light is a very powerful literary tool.

The sun can also be seen to represent our consciousness as it brings light to what was previously dark. It could even be seen as representing us in our highest form. We sometimes express this symbolism through art. One of my favorite paintings is *The Philosopher* by Rembrandt. In it, you see a wise old man sitting by a window as the light from the sun shines onto him, bringing him enlightenment.

When we stare at the sun with our human eyes, it blinds us. Yet the light of God is described as "bright as 10,000 suns," and yet you can stare right at him without being blinded? Our souls are able to see and sense so much more than our human body allows. It's no wonder people have a hard time describing their NDEs to us. Our senses are so restricted by comparison.

Death is not something to be feared. We should look forward to the day that we return home, but we first must fulfill our destiny here. Remember these lessons that the brave and wonderful near-death survivors have shared with us. Words put boundaries on things, so keep an open mind and an open heart. We are beautiful beings of light who made a choice to come here for a while to flex and grow our souls through human experiences. It's also important to remember that we are not just here solely for learning. Our time on Earth is brief, so enjoy life, have fun, and try not to take things too seriously.

Whatever life throws at you, be the light whose love and kindness ripple through the universe.

Acknowledgements

I would like to thank my wonderful family for their loving support and encouragement throughout the entire writing process. There is my lovely wife, Kate, who is also my best friend and my sweet remembrancer. She saw in me the strength to be anything and do anything. I also want to thank my three beautiful children: Emily, Sean, and Ryan. They have been my teachers, reminding me to be patient, understanding, and to always choose love above all else. There is my mom, Patricia, who was the official beta reader of my book through several rounds of drafts. She has always inspired me to reach for my dreams.

Finally, to the many brave souls who were kind enough to share their amazing experiences with me and the world. Thank you all so much!

About the Author

Brian Picchi is a consultant, software developer, and researcher of near-death studies. He has applied his background in science and psychology to help explain this phenomenon in clear, logical language. Brian holds a Bachelor's Degree in Psychology from San Diego State University, with his concentration in Neuropsychology. He is also a lifelong student of popular science, history, and astronomy.

References

CHAPTER ONE: History and Introduction

1. "Shells and ochre in Middle Paleolithic Qafzeh Cave, Israel: indications for modern behavior," accessed May 2022, https://www.sciencedirect.com/science/article/abs/pii/S00 47248408002340? via%3Dihub.

2. "Transitions Before the Transition," accessed May 2022, https://books.google.com/books?id=PjIvb55PxbcC.

3. "Direct radiocarbon dates for the Mid Upper Paleolithic (eastern Gravettian) burials from Sunghir, Russia," accessed May 2022, https://link.springer.com/article/10.1007%2Fs13219-011-0044-4.

4. George Gallup, Jr. and William Proctor, *Adventures in Immortality* (McGraw-Hill, 1982).

5. "Prevalence of Near-Death Experiences in Australia," accessed May 2022, https://digital.library.unt.edu/ark:/67531/metadc799274/m2/1/high_res_d/vol24-no2-109.pdf.

6. "One in 10 People Have 'Near-Death' Experiences," accessed May 2022, https://healthmanagement.org/c/cardio/news/one-in-10-people-have-near-death-experiences.

7. Penny Sartori, *The Near-Death Experiences of Hospitalized Intensive Care Patients* (Edwin Mellen Pr; 1 edition, 2008).

8. "Near Death Experience - In The Realm of God," accessed May 2022, https://www.youtube.com/watch?v=Nzz-nG5pjFg.

9. "Present! - Jang Jaswal's Near-Death Experience," accessed May 2022, https://www.youtube.com/watch?v=eobvYMNPmRc.

10. "Present! - Scott Taylor: A Shared Near-Death Experience," accessed May 2022, https://www.youtube.com/watch?v=2HTdyDCuY90.

11. "Near-Death Experience; God Grants Favor," accessed May 2022, https://www.youtube.com/watch?v=mx9uqlxThyE&t=1s.

CHAPTER TWO: The Out-of-Body Experience

1. "Present - Dr. Rajiv Parti's NDE," accessed May 2022, https://www.youtube.com/watch? v=7l-nbk_8EII.

2. "Carl Jung's Near Death Experience," accessed May 2022, https://carljungdepthpsychologysite.blog/2020/02/23/carl-jungs-near-death-experience-3/#.YfFepviIZPY.

3. "In a Blue Origin Rocket, William Shatner Finally Goes to Space.," accessed May 2022, https://www.nytimes.com/2021/10/13/science/william-shatner-space-blue-origin.html.

4. "I was blind but died and saw heaven - The near death experience of Vicki Umipeg Noratuk," accessed May 2022, https://www.youtube.com/watch? v=GNjRWMStgSU.

5. "Do you believe? Near-death experience survivor recalls 'amazing' encounter," accessed May 2022, https://www.today.com/health/near-death-experience-survivor-recalls-amazing-encounter-t105964.

6. Erika Hayasaki, *The Death Class: A True Story About Life* (Simon & Schuster, 2014).

7. "Present! - Robert Bare's Near-Death Experience,"

accessed May 2022, https://www.youtube.com/watch? v=gqyOWwjfMgU.

8. "The Blue Sneaker: Kimberly Clark Sharp at IANDS 2018," accessed May 2022, https://www.youtube.com/watch? v=w3ASmyyVgQY.

9. "Raymond Moody: Reincarnation," accessed May 2022, https://www.youtube.com/watch? v=n_S8yacTRnU.

10. "Near-Death Experience – Jesus Touched My Shoulder," accessed May 2022, https://www.youtube.com/watch?v=Ux1XNZ5LBWg.

11. Jeff Olsen, *I Knew Their Hearts: The Amazing True Story of a Journey Beyond the Veil to Learn the Silent Language of the Heart* (Cedar Fort, Inc., 2013).

12. "AWARE—AWAreness during REsuscitation—A prospective study," accessed May 2022, https://www.sciencedirect.com/science/article/abs/pii/S03 00957214007394.

CHAPTER THREE: The Light at the End of the Tunnel

1. Phil Donahue, "Phil Donahue Show," interviews with Jackie Pflug, Tom Sawyer, Vi Horton, Steve Price, Kristle Merzlock, Melvin Morse, Raymond Moody, *Donahue*, WGN, 1988.

2. Chris French, "Near-Death Experiences in Cardiac Arrest Survivors," *Progress in Brain Research*, 150, (2005): 351-367.

3. Raymond Moody, *Glimpses of Eternity: An Investigation Into Shared Death Experiences* (Rider, 2011).

4. "Present! - Linda Jacquin and the Near Death Experience," accessed May 2022, https://www.youtube.com/watch?v=moNG8-COKsg.

5. "Present! - Scott Taylor."

CHAPTER FOUR: Family Reunions

1. "Brian Miller, dead for 45 minutes, talks about seeing

'heaven'," accessed May 2022,
https://www.youtube.com/watch? v=OlyABe2fmcQ.
    2. Todd Burpo and Lynn Vincent, *Heaven is for Real: A Little Boy's Astounding Story of His Trip to Heaven and Back* (Thomas Nelson, 2010).
    3. Eben Alexander, *Proof of Heaven: A Neurosurgeon's Journey* (Simon & Schuster, 2012).
    4. Oprah Winfrey, "Teen's Near-Death Experience at Age 7: My 'Guardian Angel' Helped Me," interviews with Crystal Merzlock, Michelle Wilson, Wes Chandler, *The Oprah Winfrey Show*, 1990, https://www.youtube.com/watch? v=eruoYiTmkjI.

CHAPTER FIVE: This Is Heaven

    1. "Colors of GOD: Near Death Experience of Betty Cone | NDE Radio," accessed May 2022, https://soundcloud.com/brahmakumaris-bk/colors-of-god-near-death-experience-of-betty-cone-nde-radio.
    2. "Pronounced Dead for 20 Minutes - What He Saw and How it Changed His Life Forever," accessed May 2022, https://www.youtube.com/watch? v=a8jcNBVWJyE.
    3. Joel Ibrahim Kreps, *The Search for Muslim Near-Death Experiences* (2019) https://www.researchgate.net/publication/332835301_Essential_features_of_eight_published_Muslim_near-death_experiences_An_addendum_to_Joel_Ibrahim_Kreps%27s_The_search_for_Muslim_near-death_experiences.
    4. "Near Death Experience | A Mothers Love | Karen," accessed May 2022, https://www.youtube.com/watch? v=jT5r8-1kOpk.
    5. "Near Death Experience - In The Realm of God."
    6. "Present - Dr. Rajiv Parti's NDE."
    7. "Man Says He Went to Hell and Back," accessed May 2022, https://www.youtube.com/watch?v=rkFGrxzJz7o.
    8. "Near-death experiences," accessed May 2022, https://www.youtube.com/watch?v=jBiNXl9bfXc.

CHAPTER SIX: Meeting God and the Life Review

1. Jeff Olsen, *I Knew Their Hearts*.
2. "Near Death Experience - Meets God," accessed May 2022, https://www.youtube.com/watch? v=NPabMyVvC9s.
3. Lana Wachowski and Lilly Wachowski (Directors). (1999). *The Matrix* [Film]. Warner Bros. Pictures.
4. Erica McKenzie, *Dying To Fit In* (Erica McKenzie, 2015).
5. Andy Petro, *Alive in the Light - Remembering Eternity* (Outskirts Press, 2014).
6. "Present! - Robert Bare's Near-Death Experience."
7. "His Life Review Revealed A Secret | Near-Death Experience - Evert Ter Beek," accessed May 2022, https://www.youtube.com/watch? v=2Oz98Aoaaf0.

CHAPTER SEVEN: Religion

1. Jack Kerouac, *On the Road* (Viking Press, 1957).
2. Melvin Morse and Paul Perry, *Closer to the Light: Learning from the Near-Death Experiences of Children: Amazing Revelations of What It Feels Like to Die* (Ivy Books, 1991).
3. Craig R. Lundahl, Ph.D., *Angels in Near-Death Experiences* (1992) https://digital.library.unt.edu/ark:/67531/metadc798908/m2/1/high_res_d/vol11-no1-49.pdf.
4. Cassandra Musgrave, *The Near-Death Experience: A Study of Spiritual Transformation* (1997) https://digital.library.unt.edu/ark:/67531/metadc799346/m2/1/high_res_d/vol15-no3-187.pdf.
5. "Billy Graham South African Crusade 1973," accessed May 2022, https://www.youtube.com/watch? v=HTHxivBCahA.
6. "Colors of GOD: Near Death Experience of Betty Cone | NDE Radio," accessed May 2022,

https://soundcloud.com/brahmakumaris-bk/colors-of-god-near-death-experience-of-betty-cone-nde-radio.

7. "Present! - Jang Jaswal's Near-Death Experience."

8. "Present - Dr. Rajiv Parti's NDE."

9. "Near-Death Experience among Iranian Muslim Cardiopulmonary Resuscitation Survivors," accessed May 2022, https://pubmed.ncbi.nlm.nih.gov/33344213/.

10. "Afterlife Insurance," accessed May 2022, https://www.chabad.org/multimedia/video_cdo/aid/1749369/jewish/Afterlife-Insurance.htm.

11. Randy Kay, *Dying to Meet Jesus: How Encountering Heaven Changed My Life* (Chosen Books, 2020).

12. "Near-Death Experience, Asks to See The Christ," https://www.youtube.com/watch? v=lShjrg3M7Ro.

CHAPTER EIGHT: The Seeds of Time

1. "Present! - Robert Bare's Near-Death Experience," accessed May 2022, https://www.youtube.com/watch? v=gqyOWwjfMgU.

2. Jerry Zucker (Director). (1990). *Ghost* [Film]. Paramount Pictures.

3. Mary C. Neal, *A Doctor's Extraordinary Account of Her Death, Heaven, Angels, and Life Again: a True Story* (WaterBrook, 2012).

4. "Near Death Experience - In The Realm of God."

5. "Paul McCartney Carpool Karaoke," accessed May 2022, https://www.youtube.com/watch? v=QjvzCTqkBDQ.

6. "Afterlife Insurance."

7. Craig R. Lundahl, Ph.D., *Near-Death Visions of Unborn Children: Indications of a Pre-Earth Life* (1992) https://digital.library.unt.edu/ark:/67531/metadc798997/m2/1/high_res_d/vol11-no2-123.pdf.

8. "Billy Graham and Larry King January 1988," accessed May 2022, https://www.youtube.com/watch? v=wMUhnCJln1A.

9. "Raymond Moody: Near-Death Experience as a

Gateway to the Afterlife," accessed May 2022, https://www.youtube.com/watch? v=6AY-A16a-4I.

10. "Erica McKenzie NDE talk 2016," accessed May 2022, https://www.youtube.com/watch?v=K6udn-HTleM.

11. H.G. Wells, *The Time Machine* (William Heinemann, 1895).

12. Kim Ki-duk (Director). (2003). *Spring, Summer, Fall, Winter…Spring* [Film]. Korea Pictures.

CHAPTER NINE: Past Lives

1. Emilie Ardolino (Director). (1989). *Chances Are* [Film]. TriStar Pictures.

2. Jim B. Tucker, M.D., *Life Before Life: Children's Memories of Previous Lives* (St. Martin's Griffin, 2005).

3. Bruce Leininger and Andrea Leininger, *Soul Survivor: The Reincarnation of a World War II Fighter Pilot* (Grand Central Publishing, 2010).

4. "Evidence of Reincarnation in Childhood by Dr. Jim Tucker (Full Presentation)," accessed May 2022, https://www.youtube.com/watch? v=La8vG4mA0is.

5. Brian L. Weiss, *Many Lives, Many Masters: The True Story of a Prominent Psychiatrist, His Young Patient, and the Past-Life Therapy That Changed Both Their Lives* (Fireside, 1988).

6. The Oprah Winfrey Show, "Dr. Brian Weiss Uses Past-Life Regression for Jodi's Fear of Dolls," (2008) https://www.youtube.com/watch? v=MD9ZXRc0X3o.

7. Phil Donahue, interviews (1988).

8. Rajiv Parti M.D., *Dying to Wake Up: A Doctor's Voyage into the Afterlife and the Wisdom He Brought Back* (Atria Books, 2017).

9. Carl Sagan, Ann Druyan, and Steven Soter, *Cosmos: A Personal Voyage* (1980).

10. "Raymond Moody talks about Children and Past Life Memories," accessed May 2022, https://www.youtube.com/watch?v=ZaHcnSOYrgc.

CHAPTER TEN: Gifts from the Other Side

1. "Over & Back – Near Death Experiences," *The Geraldo Rivera Show,* created by Geraldo Rivera, Tribune Entertainment, 1988.

2. "Present! - Robert Bare's Near-Death Experience."

3. "Colors of GOD: Near Death Experience of Betty Cone."

4. "Near-Death Experience; God Grants Favor."

5. "A Prospectively Studied Near-Death Experience with Corroborated Out-of-Body Perceptions and Unexplained Healing," accessed May 2022, https://digital.library.unt.edu/ark:/67531/metadc799351/m2/1/high_res_d/vol25-no2-69.pdf.

6. "Lloyd Rudy interview on Near Death Experiences," accessed May 2022, https://www.youtube.com/watch?v=NdPDNXc3mp8.

7. "Near-Death Experience – Jesus Touched My Shoulder."

CHAPTER ELEVEN: Where Science Meets Fiction

1. John Carpenter (Director). (1984). *Starman* [Film]. Columbia Pictures.

2. "Immortality: Can we upload human consciousness? | Michio Kaku, Michael Shermer & more | Big Think," accessed May 2022, https://www.youtube.com/watch?v=E3FRtUTFZuk.

3. "What Are Little Girls Made Of?" *Star Trek*, created by Gene Roddenberry, Season 1, Episode 7, Desilu Productions, 1966.

4. "StarTalk Radio Show," accessed May 2022, https://www.startalkradio.net.

5. Barbara Honegger, *The OBE as a Near-Birth Experience.* In Roll, W. G., Beloff, J., and White, R. A. (Eds.). *Research in Parapsychology.* Scarecrow Press. pp. 230-231. (1983).

CHAPTER TWELVE: Conclusions and Practical

Applications

1. "Near-Death Experience; God Grants Favor."
2. Mahatma Gandhi, *The Collected Works of Mahatma Gandhi-Volume XIII* (Mahatma Gandhi, 1913).
3. "Erica McKenzie, *Dying To Fit In*"
4. Martin Luther King, Jr., "I Have a Dream by Martin Luther King, Jr.; August 28, 1963." The Avalon Project, Yale Law School, 2008,
avalon.law.yale.edu/20th_century/mlk01.asp.

Made in United States
North Haven, CT
28 May 2022

19630200R00088